1996

KOREA:
A WORLD IN C

Edited by
Kenneth W. Thompson

Volume VIII
In the Miller Center Series on
A World in Change

UNIVERSITY
PRESS OF
AMERICA

Lanham • New York • London

The Miller Center

University of Virginia

Copyright © 1996 by
University Press of America,® Inc.
4720 Boston Way
Lanham, Maryland 20706

3 Henrietta Street
London WC2E 8LU England

Copublished by arrangement with
The Miller Center of Public Affairs,
University of Virginia

The views expressed by the author(s) of this publication do not necessarily represent the opinions of the Miller Center. We hold to Jefferson's dictum that: "Truth is the proper and sufficient antagonist to error, and has nothing to fear from the conflict, unless by human interposition, disarmed of her natural weapons, free argument and debate."

ISBN: 0-7618-0266-5 (cloth: alk. ppr.)
ISBN: 0-7618-0267-3 (pbk: alk. ppr.)

⊖™ The paper used in this publication meets the minimum requirements of American National Standard for Information Sciences—Permanence of Paper for Printed Library Materials, ANSI Z39.48–1964.

To the Generation of
Hyoung-Chan Choe and Youngho Kim
and
To Robert J. Myers

Contents

Preface

The Miller Center volume on Korea is the eighth in a series entitled "A World in Change." Especially in the post-Cold War era, it is important for two reasons to note regions where potential change is most likely. First, change often brings conflict as the parties contend over the nature and character of change. What forms of change are acceptable to the parties and what forms will be fought over either in realizing or opposing the change? Second, change involves movement and progress toward a set of goals and objectives. It is the means of achieving national purposes. Change may lead to hard won gain or maintenance of the status quo.

Korea was divided in two by the Soviet Union and the United States much as it had been occupied and divided by China, Japan, and Russia in the past. Therefore, it is important that we measure the forces at work for unification in the future and those that resist unification. Democracy and horizontal equality are part of the drive for unity, but their absence in North Korea makes unity more difficult. What are the lessons of unification between the two Germanies? What are the difficulties? What has been the Korean experience in the past five years? What are the political, economic, and social conditions in the two Koreas? The questions will help us determine the prospects for unity and democracy in the coming years.

Introduction

A treatise on the future of Korea requires perspectives on both the north and the south. It calls for the examination of questions concerning Korea and Asia, Korea and the world, the Korean War, U.S.-Korean relations, North Korea, and nuclear weapons in North Korea and other countries in Asia. These questions frame the discussion that follows and lead to analysis and the projection of trends and developments into the future.

Robert J. Myers has devoted a lifetime to the study of Asia and more recently to the unfolding of democracy around the world. He inaugurates this series, as he inspired the preparation of this volume, with a discussion of "Change in Asia." The focus of his essay is Korea, the Philippines, and the United States. Myers is both a theorist and practitioner. He attempts to promote democracy through projects such as the Asian Center for the Study of Democratic Institutions in the Philippines. Democracy is the core idea that runs through Dr. Myers' presentation. He presents guideposts for the evolution of democracy in Asia. He clarifies the debate over presidential and cabinet government. He looks hard at the division of political strength between the candidates and political parties in Korea. Myers provides an excellent introduction to our subject.

In chapter two, Professor Hakjoon Kim of Dankook University reviews the current trends in international politics worldwide and in the Asian-Pacific region in particular. Significantly, some of the questions he asks parallel those posed by Dr. Myers. However, Myers challenges the triumphalist views of Francis Fukuyama. Hakjoon Kim challenges Samuel Huntington's and Paul Kennedy's views of crisis and decline. He questions whether one can be as optimistic about international economics as about international politics. Whereas he sees a "Democratic Renaissance" around the world, he notes the movement of the world economy from protectionism to regionalism. He sees merciless economic wars between regions and trade blocs in the future. Furthermore, he observes that triumphalism tends to be short-lived; he worries that this may be the case with Russia and the former Soviet Union. Yet he sees some signs of hope in Eastern Europe and in Yeltsin's Russia. In Asia, he finds reasons for both hope and anxiety. He asks why in an era of post-Cold War rapprochement, Asian countries are using massive amounts of their financial resources to augment their military power. The answer is fear that a future struggle for regional hegemony between Japan and China will involve the entire region. He leaves us with an unanswered question: Will the region and the world be swallowed up in such a struggle?

In Chapter three, Dr. Myers returns to discuss "Korea in a World of Change." I have the impression that Dr. Myers' experience in Korea surpasses that of almost every American. After noting that Korea's experience goes back several thousand years, Myers focuses attention on the post-World War II period. He divides this history into three distinct periods. The first is the nationalist period under Syngman Rhee. The second begins with the ouster of Rhee and is the era of the "garrison state." The third appears to surround the leadership of Roh Tae Woo, culminating in the administration of Kim Young Sam. Having discussed aspects of the three periods, Myers returns to the United States to reflect on the future of democracy in the United States. He concludes by discussing horizontal democracy in the United States and Korea.

Chapter four is the sole chapter devoted to the Korean War and falls in the section of that name. Youngho Kim is one of the most outstanding graduate students in the past 20 years of the Department of Government and Foreign Affairs. He is a prodigious researcher, as demonstrated by his work in the basic documents concerning the Korean War and especially the recently released Soviet documents. In grappling with issues concerning the origins of the war, Kim found that Stalin and not Kim Il Sung played the pivotal role. His chapter is the most original in the volume, setting forth conclusions that are bound to be debated by interpreters and researchers for years to come. No brief summary can do justice to the subtlety of some of his political and military analysis on Stalin's role. Alternately encouraging and holding back the North Koreans, Stalin ultimately gave the green light for the advance. Kim shows that the Soviet objective was maintaining the prestige of the Soviets and pressing forward with their policy of rolling back American influence and prestige around the world. Kim's paper merits careful study by all who would understand the "origins of the Korean War."

Chapter five is a broad historical and cultural review of U.S.-Korean relations. It reflects the analytical powers of scholar-diplomat Seung-Soo Han, South Korea's ambassador to the United States. Ambassador Han quotes a statement about Koreans from the first book written by an American on Korea:

> The Koreans are not a shop-keeping people. Shops are few in number and deficient in kind. . . . Trade is not one of the mainsprings to action in men and women in Korea.

Han traces the stages in trade and economic growth of Korea that culminated in the 1980s when Korea came to be seen as a source of capital for other countries. Korea has become the 12th largest trading nation and the 15th largest economy in the world. Korea is America's eighth largest trading partner and fifth largest importer of U.S. agricultural products. Han traces the evolution of North Korea viewed as an irrelevant anachronism to the impact of the North Korean nuclear crisis in the spring of 1994. The ambassador goes on to discuss the advantages and disadvantages of having the United States as Korea's largest trading partner from 1948 on. By the 1980s, a two-way flow of trade began to take shape. The goal has been to combine U.S. high technology with Korea's manufacturing base. Ambassador Han closes with some thoughts on reunification and the North Korean nuclear problem.

Ambassador James R. Lilley, who represented the United States in Korea (1986-89) and China (1989-91) follows Ambassador Han in this volume. His primary thesis is that if the United States can manage its relations with China, relations with North Korea will fall into place. He discusses democracy in South Korea—it still thrives today—and democracy in China after the Tiananmen massacre—it has never completely died. Ambassador Lilley offers a vivid picture of the turbulence and brutality in the Square and the harsh actions threatened or taken against the dissidents. He describes the lack of consensus on China in the United States and the dubious linkage of human rights and most-favored-nation status. (Lilley argues that those who pushed linkage knew it would not work.) Finally, he traces American attempts to work in the United Nations with China on sanctions against Saddam Hussein and on cooperation on the North Korean nuclear problem. When we placed sanctions on military transfers to China, they turned to Russia. When we pressed human rights on the Chinese, they drew closer to Singapore, Malaysia, Indonesia, and Thailand, which shared China's disapproval of the American human rights policy. Finally, Lilley notes likely friction between China and the United States over the South China Sea, modernization and expansion of the military, different cultural values, and the Chinese concept of a free market in a large socialist "bird cage." Lilley answers a series of questions about North Korea at the end of his chapter. As for China, Lilley believes a strategic partnership between China and the United States is needed. It is essential to the stability of the whole regional system in Asia.

Part IV in our volume deals with North Korea and the controversy over nuclear weapons. Ambassador Chong-Ha Yoo was Korean ambassador to the United Nations when he visited the Miller Center. He has served as vice foreign minister and has negotiated with North Korea. Yoo visited North Korea in 1991 with a group of 20 South Koreans. In part, his perspective on North Korea grew out of that experience. The North Koreans discussed the economic problem, fear of the United States, and the need to reduce their expenditures for armaments. Ambassador Yoo rehearses some of the known facts about a North Korean nuclear weapon capacity and the range of its missiles covering the whole of South Korea and potentially the industrial parts of Japan. Yoo also recites what is known concerning the crisis between the International Atomic Energy Agency and North Korea. He explains why replacement of the current graphite system reactors, similar to the Chernobyl reactors, with light-water systems would increase safely in the region. If North Korea rejects international inspections or departs from agreements that have been reached, the U.N. Security Council could apply sanctions cutting off the oil supply to North Korea or money transfers from Japan. If this happened, North Korea has announced it would consider such action tantamount to a declaration of war freeing them from obligations in the 1953 armistice agreement. As a seasoned diplomat, Ambassador Yoo provides a responsible analysis of the North Korean problem.

Mark Barry is an outstanding graduate student at the University of Virginia who has had unique opportunities to view the North Korean situation on the ground. He met North Korean President Kim Il Sung and visited North Korea twice. His dissertation focuses on U.S.-North Korean relations from 1987 to 1994. In contrast with those who concentrate on North Korea and nuclear weapons, Barry is primarily concerned with overall relations between the two states. Whereas others see a declining curve in relations, Barry finds grounds for some optimism. He points to the efforts of leaders such as former president Jimmy Carter and evangelist Billy Graham who gained the confidence of Kim Il Sung.

In the same way that South Korea and the United States have felt resentment and hatred toward the North Koreans, North Korea feels ill will because of the division of Korea, the American occupation of South Korea from 1945 to 1948, the bombing of its capital, and destruction of its industries by the Americans. Indeed, the United States is still technically at war with North Korea, there being only an armistice. Despite 33 meetings through May 1993 between American and North Korean diplomats, little progress was achieved (From 1955 to 1972, American and Chinese ambassadors met 150 times, the latter at a higher level). Early in 1993, envoys of the two countries began meeting in New York, leading to negotiations involving Assistant Secretary of State Robert Gallucci and the first vice foreign minister Kang Sok-Ju. From this point on, negotiators were able to point to some progress. Americans learned that the North Koreans resented the legalistic and aggressive approach of the IAEA. They found that what the North Koreans sought was recognition of their legitimacy. Finally, the United States offered a package deal including light-water reactors and a road map toward full diplomatic relations. Along the way South

Korea expressed opposition to being kept on the sidelines in the negotiations. Barry warns that sanctions against North Korea could lead to a nuclear arms race between China, Japan, and the Koreas. Mark Barry alone among contributors to this volume argues that North Korea has had grievances and calls for the parties to understand what concerns the other most deeply. In the case of North Korea, it is pride and lack of recognition by others. In the end, Barry believes that progress can be made in relations with North Korea.

Hakjoon Kim, the author of chapter two, discusses North Korea's nuclear weapon dispute in chapter nine. He warns that the North is serious about obtaining a nuclear weapon. Its economy is a cause of alarm to the North Korean people. Its gross national product is less than a tenth that of South Korea's. It lacks oil and food grain and is isolated internationally. Only China continues its help. Kim feels the cross-recognition of the two Koreas by the four major powers—Russia and China of South Korea and the United States and Japan of North Korea—could lead to a true peace agreement beyond the present armistice. Yet the North Koreans may insist on a continuation of their nuclear program. This could endanger the whole of the Korean Peninsula. He examines the scenarios of options for North Korea—status quo, reform, hard-line, and collapse. Kim believes that South Korea must take the initiative, but he is not sure that peace is likely except through an unexpected development in the North.

Hyoung-Chan Choe is assistant director of the North American Division II of the Ministry of Foreign Affairs in Seoul. The format of his review of North Korea's dangerous nuclear deal is an expanded version of a substantial paper he wrote for my Government and Foreign Affairs seminar at the University of Virginia. It is a history of the North Korean nuclear problem viewed from South Korea. Every stage in the unfolding crisis is explored in context. While it is true that Choe's point of view is that of a South Korean, it is also true that he leaves no detail or event unexamined. Because of its scope and character, I have made it the concluding chapter in the volume. No one who would study the North Korean problem can escape the responsibility of revisiting step-by-step the events leading up to the crisis we have witnessed.

No one who would talk of the future can ignore the past, which Mr. Choe as an official of one of the parties reconstructs for our study and reasoned judgment.

I.

KOREA IN A
WORLD IN CHANGE

CHAPTER ONE

Change in Asia: Developments in Korea, the Philippines, and the United States*

ROBERT J. MYERS

NARRATOR: One part of the world where change seems to be especially dramatic is Asia. I remember lectures at this university and at the Miller Center in which people would utter such phrases as "there will never be a Jefferson in China," implying that in Asia, culture, history, and social structures would always be obstacles to the development of democracy.

Dr. Robert Myers has been very active in exploring, encouraging, and assisting in the development of democracy and a better society in a number of Asian countries. He is responsible for the leadership and the formulation of a $5 million program for agricultural and industrial development in the Philippines. He has taken the lead in other areas throughout his career as publisher of *The New Republic*, as co-founder of *The Washingtonian*, as a member of the Office of Strategic Services, and as a public servant in the State Department and the Defense Department.

Since 1980 Dr. Myers has been president of the Carnegie Council on Ethics and International Affairs. He has taken hold of that organization and given it new life. It was founded by Andrew Carnegie in 1914. Its history reflects significant stages in its development. Perhaps of all of its stages, the current one is the

---

Presented in a Forum at the Miller Center of Public Affairs on 12 September 1991.

most vital and creative—in the publication of an annual journal on ethics and international affairs, in a related series of lecture and study programs at universities around the country, and in an active program in New York City in a beautiful new facility that Dr. Myers has made possible for the Carnegie Council.

MR. MYERS: A couple of years ago our Council established a center in the Philippines called the Asian Center for the Study of Democratic Institutions. Next year it will be renamed the Corazon Aquino Center for the Study of Democratic Institutions. When she retires, Mrs. Aquino will become president of the center.

In trying to promote democracy in Asia, we are perfectly aware that there is no one particular kind of democracy, yet all democracies have something in common. A few years ago at the Council, Jacques Barzun gave a talk entitled "Is Democratic Theory for Export?" His answer, of course, was a resounding *no*. There is no theory of democracy; rather, there is more of a democratic theorem based on various writings of the Founding Fathers, such as the Declaration of Independence and other documents of this nature.

We are not really trying to impose a particular democratic model on the Asians, but it has been encouraging to see that many of these countries that were authoritarian or communist—and in some cases both—have been making substantial changes. I intend to outline some of these changes.

We have tried to develop guideposts on how democracy gets started in Asia. I suppose we have worked more on Korea than on other Asian countries. We just had our fourth conference in Seoul at the end of June on Progress in Korean Democracy. We worked there with the Asiatic Research Center.

The growth of democracy seems to go through four stages. First, you have to have a reasonable amount of stability. Second, you have to have economic development, which can itself be a very destabilizing activity. It is ironic, for example, that in the People's Republic of China the antique leadership is convinced that stability is the only principle of government that makes any sense, while all around them furious economic activity and development is literally changing the society, even though the leadership doesn't seem to know it.

The third point is that if you have economic development going on, you normally have participation by the population in government. Korea is a good example of the growing popular participation in government.

Finally, you have to have some notion of social justice. You must have some kind of program that keeps all of these active, well-educated people involved in the society. Korea, from that perspective, has made a great deal of progress. Obviously, the thing most people think of is economic progress, but even Lee Kuan Yew in Singapore finally has conceded that if you have substantial economic development like you have in Singapore, you cannot keep all of the people out of the government despite the desire to have a one-party state. For Lee Kuan Yew the support of 60 percent of the population is not enough; he wants everyone to support his party.

That was the attitude in Korea until 1988, when Roh Tae Woo was elected president. They had to make a lot of concessions on party nominations and on having direct elections, which they had not held before.

The problem that the Koreans now face in trying to develop a reasonable political democracy is whether they want to have a presidential system, as provided for in the current constitution for the Sixth Republic, or whether they want to have a cabinet system. Maybe this doesn't sound like a great distinction, so let me explain how it works. A presidential system generally works best if you only have two parties; hence the president is elected with a majority vote. In Korea there are a number of parties—at least three or four—that contest the presidency. Consequently, when Roh Tae Woo was elected in February of 1988, he received 36 percent of the vote. Two other opponents received about 26 percent each, and the rest were scattered around.

The practical effect of this election was that the ruling party, the Democratic Justice party, for the first time did not control the National Assembly, a very awkward situation for the ruling party. In the United States we are used to divided government. Be it good or bad, we have a president from one party and a Congress controlled by another, and we have learned to muddle along somehow.

The Koreans, however, grew impatient with this kind of system and decided in effect what amounted to a constitutional coup in January 1990. The three conservative parties of Roh Tae Woo, Kim Young Sam, and Kim Jong Pil were merged, which gave them about 80 percent of the National Assembly vote. The voters, in effect, having voted for these three different people, found that they had gotten the same guy. The merger of these parties was so enormously unpopular that the Democratic Justice party, now called the Democratic Liberal party (which is the conservative party), has sunk in the polls to something less than 15 percent popularity. And elections are scheduled for next year.

Should Korea continue the presidential system, it appears that again there will be at least three or four presidential candidates. Roh Tae Woo cannot succeed himself. The person who is supposed to run is Kim Young Sam, but the party apparently is unwilling to give him the nomination. Kim Young Sam's only recourse then will be to start another party, which should not be difficult since the Democratic Liberal party has less than 15 percent support and Kim Young Sam got 26 percent of the vote in the last election. If he runs there will be two conservative candidates. I don't know who the other candidate will be—perhaps Kim Jong Pil, the former prime minister under President Park.

The other merger to try to conquer the conservatives involves Kim Dae Jung, the long time oppositionist, and Lee Ke Taek. They have merged into a party called the Democratic party. As a result, at least two conservative candidates will run, at least one independent, and possibly a fourth candidate.

It is almost guaranteed, then, that in Korea—and this is a very similar problem in the Philippines—there will be a minority-elected president. This, of course, is a difficult way to try to run a democracy.

The current economic crisis in Korea overshadows that country's political situation. Most of us don't associate Korea with any economic problems, but they surely have them. Its balance of payments through July 1991 was a $7.8 billion deficit, 70 percent of that to Japan. It has begun a campaign against foreign imports—a typical mercantilist proposition that will obviously hurt the United States, particularly in terms of imports.

Korea has a growth rate of 9.1 percent in the economy, but given its 10 percent inflation rate, it really isn't doing all that well. The Koreans' big problem, which they haven't faced, is the need to retool and restructure a lot of industry, and that will take a good deal of capital investment.

Their exports are not competitive, particularly in automobiles, where they made such a splash. They have not been able to sell the Hyundai here. Their automobile industry is in further trouble because of a break in the longtime arrangement between General Motors and Dai Woo Manufacturing Company to assemble Pontiacs in Korea. Apparently, this relationship is going to come to an end.

All of these kinds of problems are going to make the political race next year rather bitter. A lot of these candidates tend to be representatives of particular geographical areas, which is rather remarkable for a country as small as Korea. Korean regionalism has persisted despite instant communications, newspapers, and all of the technology that normally unite a country. This means that there will probably be even more political candidates, and their issues will be not only economic and regional, but may also involve a certain amount of personalism.

Aristotle advised that if you want to have a constitutional government, you shouldn't often change the constitution. The Koreans don't seem to pay much attention to Aristotle. So, I think they will have to decide in the next constitution what sort of government they are going to have.

Another country that for a long time has been democratic in form, but less so in substance, is the Philippines. They also have a presidential system and usually have at least three or four candidates. Unless they can do something to narrow the number of contenders, they, too, will elect someone by a minority. There is also talk there about whether they should address this problem through a cabinet system.

As you know, Mrs. Aquino, to everyone's surprise, has done quite an outstanding job. She has a reputation for having brought back the democratic process to the Philippines, imperfect as it may be. The biggest complaint about her is that it is very hard to get anything done in the Philippines, economically and so on. The reason for that is she actually lets the government work!

Instead of going to the Marcos palace to obtain a government permit, you must now go through official government channels. In this manner, President Aquino has broken up a lot of the old power bases and made the government more significant, even though it isn't as efficient as it might be. Still, I think she has a lot to be proud of in that regard.

The opposition to President Aquino is basically the Nationalist party, led by Salvador Laurel, whose father was the president under the Japanese, and Juan Ponce Enrile, Mrs. Aquino's former minister of defense. Finally, Mrs. Aquino is opposed by her cousin, José Cojuangco. Enrile and Cojuangco benefitted greatly under the Marcos regime and are reputedly the two richest people in the Philippines.

General Fidel Ramos, who resigned a few months ago as minister of defense, is considered the leading candidate. Assuming Mrs. Aquino supports him, he will represent the Peoples' Power Movement, which is not really a party but rather a political movement.

No one used to care whether President Aquino would support the next president, because they didn't think she would stay or that she would have that type of influence. But she is now much sought after to give her blessing to Fidel Ramos. Ramos will be facing the three Nationalist party leaders and Senate President Jovito Solonga, who will run under a new party.

The problem in the Philippines is in some ways deeper than the one in Korea on this multicandidate problem because all of the senators run on a national basis. In other words, the top 23 vote getters in the Philippines are elected to the senate, rather than by regional representation. So, 23 potential candidates will leap into the race if they feel the call.

One of the complicating problems for democracy in the short term is the base agreement that you are probably reading about in the newspaper. It is supposed to be decided no later than 16 September. It has to be approved by two-thirds of the senate, that is, 16 of its 23 members.

Right now there are 12 senators against the base agreement and 11 for it. Mrs. Aquino, of course, is supporting the base agreement, so there appears to be a genuine standoff. The arguments against the base agreement are typically nationalistic and, of course, to some extent anti-American. On the other hand, you have someone like Enrile who is against the base agreement only because Mrs. Aquino is for it. Whether anything will be done that can save it, I don't know.

The real issue is whether they will turn down the $250 million a year the Americans are offering, along with at least 20,000 jobs related to the base. But more important, without the American military bases in the Philippines, people will not be very enthused about investing money there. Investors may be incorrect in their thinking; certainly they are more worried than I am about the New Peoples' Army, which they are afraid will take over the country when the Americans pull out. I think the threat of this happening has been exaggerated for many years and for many good reasons, but none-theless, this perception continues. So people will look upon the Philippines as a poor investment—which they more or less do now, anyway—making it hard to attract the kind of capital the Philippines needs.

In 1960 the Koreans and the Filipinos had the same level of income, and now Korean incomes are approximately 10 times those of the Philippines. Much of the blame lies in Marcos's mishandling and looting of the country, but nonetheless, it is a tough situation.

There are many options, of course, on the bases. It is not quite as final as it might seem if they really do turn it down. I suppose you could subcontract Subic Bay to repair boats, for example, so the whole affair may end a little differently from what is now envisioned.

I will say a few words about Japan before we turn to Taiwan. I think that by 27 October the LDP, the Liberal Democratic party (it's marvelous how all of these conservatives adopt names like Liberal Democratic, or in Korea, Democratic Liberal) will have decided if they want to keep Prime Minister Kaifu. In Japan, the Liberal Democratic party has been in power since 1953. Their longevity has been aided by an opposition that calls itself the Japan Socialist party. This party, of course, was not defeated by

9

conservative ideas; it was defeated by the roaring economic success of Japan. The Liberal Democratic party has always been short on ideas, but it hasn't needed any: If Japan prospers, the LDP prospers. The Japan Socialist party has now changed its name to the Democratic Socialistic party, but I don't think that is going to do them much good. The real action still is in the Liberal Democratic party, and the question is whether Kaifu will again be elected prime minister by the party bosses. There is a good chance that he will be reelected, because although party members publicly claim to dislike Kaifu's weakness, in fact he is exactly what they want. They don't want a prime minister who is overly decisive, but rather prefer that nothing much happens. That has been very much to their benefit in international relations. They can always respond late and little. The only individual who seems to be a real contender for the prime ministership is Kiichi Miyazawa, the former finance minister who now has the largest faction.

Keeping the same group in power so long has had a deleterious effect on the quality of Japanese democracy. There are roughly 600 elected seats, and 25 percent of those seats are in effect inherited. They are like gold club memberships from father to son, because they come from a small district where one family dominates politics. I don't know if this bothers the Japanese. At any rate, that is what they have done, and this family control of political seats is getting tighter.

A great split will occur some day in the Liberal Democratic party because it has obvious factions. They have three main factions now. Furthermore, there are issues in Japan that are not addressed—for example, the traditional arguments between producers and consumers, which so far the producers have always won, although there aren't very many of them.

There are big questions about Japan's place in the world. Are they going to revitalize their foreign policy and play a bigger role in Asia and elsewhere? Are they going to continue to sit back as best they can and let economic machinery work in their favor? There are also big issues concerning infrastructure. For example, the country needs a lot of building up of highways and certainly a sewage system, but so far Japan is not spending a lot of money on infrastructure. There are also environmental issues of importance.

10

Finally, there is Taiwan. I tend to be rather biased about Taiwan and am in favor of what has happened there over the last 40 years. When I first went there in 1950 during the Korean War, Taiwan was a real disaster. Nationalist troops had come there from Shanghai and had a terrible relationship with the Taiwanese. There had been a massacre in February 1947, after which martial law was imposed. Everyone was trying to leave the island. Until the Korean War started in June 1950, no one with any assets wanted to stay; everyone wanted to get out. Now, of course, Taiwan has a considerably different financial image.

In terms of democracy, I think Taiwan has done well in terms of the traditional Bill of Rights sort of freedoms. Their political system is such that the ruling government party allows political opposition, and in the last election the ruling government party got something like 60 percent of the votes. So there seems to be a possibility that political pluralism will eventually work there.

Various attempts are underway to bring Taiwanese-style democracy and capitalism into mainland China. A look at the trade figures shows that at least in some respects they have been successful. Taiwan has been investing heavily in southern China, and the exports from China, which in a sense are Taiwanese, have reached something like $12 billion, up $5 or $6 billion from last year. This investment of time and capital is developing southern China in a most amazing way.

I have always thought there might be something to what Mao Zedong used to say, namely, at least 5 percent of the Chinese people were irrevocably reactionaries. What they are now longing for is more opportunity. I feel that the growth of economic, social, and political opportunities in Taiwan—compared to when I was first there in the 1950s—has been rather remarkable. Indeed, their $75 billion in foreign reserves will give them opportunities for new infrastructure work, which is as badly needed in Taiwan as it is in Japan. The Taiwanese seem set to build a subway and other infrastructures. I will close with that generalization.

NARRATOR: Our first commentator will be Mr. Lin. Mr. Lin is a good example of the aspirations of the government department and the Miller Center to have a new generation of scholars. He is

11

currently at what is perhaps the most distinguished center for historical and political studies in all of Asia, the Academica Sinica, where for a number of generations great scholarly work has been done.

MR. LIN: I will talk a little bit about Taiwanese diplomatic relations in international society. As you may know, Taiwan was ousted from the United Nations in 1971 when mainland China joined that body. Taiwan remains a member of the Asian Development Bank.

Taiwan is the 13th largest trading economy in the world and the sixth largest trading partner of the United States, but Taiwan has almost no important role in international society, particularly in international organizations. People on the island, particularly opposition party members, want Taiwan to rejoin the United Nations. Of course, it is very difficult for Taiwan because the People's Republic of China is going to veto Taiwan's entrance to the United Nations. Taiwan may still attempt to get a seat in the United Nations, particularly since for the first time, North and South Korea agreed to have separate entrance into the United Nations. Thus, the people in Taiwan do want much greater international recognition.

Taiwan has a six-year development plan beginning in 1991, amounting to about $300 billion. The plan focuses on infrastructure, including a new expressway, a petrochemical plant, and a power plant. Many European ministers have visited Taiwan in the past few months because they want to do business with Taiwan.

There has been much interaction between Taiwan and China since 1977. In 1979, there was only $80 million in trade between Taiwan and China, but by 1991 there were billions in direct trade. One million Taiwanese have visited China, and when they visit, they realize the real situation on the mainland, particularly after the 4 June 1989 Tiananmen Square incident. Recent public opinion polls show that 10 to 20 percent of Taiwanese people favor independence.

George Kennan argued in 1948 and 1949 that the best future for Taiwan lay in self-determination for the people of the island. When the Korean War broke out, the Truman and then the

Eisenhower administrations stuck to a one-China principle, but this one-China principle began to change in the Kennedy and Johnson administrations. Finally Nixon tried to normalize relations with China. In 1972, in the Shanghai Communique, the United States government stated that Taiwan was a part of China.

Taiwanese independence remains a very touchy issue. More and more Taiwanese want to have a separate state, not simply a local branch of the government of the People's Republic of China. Of course, for the United States government, this may be a very difficult issue in the years ahead.

The representatives of U.S.-based, Taiwan independence movements are moving back to Taiwan to help Taiwan and its people build a new country. If Taiwan declares independence, then the Beijing government may use military means against Taiwan. In the years ahead, this will continue to be a touchy issue among Beijing, Taipei, and Washington.

NARRATOR: Professor S. C. Leng is the architect of a number of programs at the University of Virginia and across the nation. He has been president of the American Association of Chinese Studies. He has been the longtime chairman of Asian Studies at the University of Virginia. He is the Dorothy Danforth Compton Professor at the Miller Center. We feel very privileged, as we try to broaden the geographic perspective of the Miller Center, that Professor Leng has taken the lead in that regard.

MR. LENG: I was very impressed by Dr. Myers' perceptive analysis of the countries in question. I agree that President Aquino has done very well. Recently, I was in the Philippines and I got the impression that the major complaint about her is that she seems to have surrounded herself with her relatives. I see her doing the same thing that Chiang Kai-shek did. He was a good man, but unfortunately he surrounded himself with the wrong people.

I want to move on to Mr. Lin's remarks. I differ with him on the particularly touchy issue of Taiwan's independence. At this point in history, any efforts to assert independence will be destabilizing to East Asia. The best Taiwan can do is to maintain the current status quo and to seek from mainland China treatment of Taiwan as an equal entity, without getting into the formality of an independent Taiwanese state. Taiwan should press Beijing to allow Taiwan to enter international organizations, regardless of the official name Taiwan uses. Their basic aim should be to maintain the current status quo and continue the contacts with mainland China that Dr. Myers described. Taiwan should not sell itself short. President Lee Teng-hui can be the Boris Yeltsin of China; Taiwan can be the Russia of China. Through contacts, through investment, and through the example of democracy, Taiwan can play a very significant role in China. There is no reason for Taiwan to rush into independence. As indicated, at most only 20 percent of Taiwan's population favors independence. Still, Taiwan has no love for communism in China; certainly there is no need for Taiwan to be unified with the mainland.

The point is that if the Taiwanese attempt an independence movement, supposedly China will declare a blockade and send a few missiles toward Taiwan. If this happens, the entire economic structure of Taiwan will collapse. This is certainly not in our interest, in Taiwan's interest, or in the interest of East Asia.

My argument, then, is that we should maintain the status quo and try to press China not to undermine Taiwan's effort to reenter the international arena. At the same time, Taiwan must continue the democratic process and economic development. In the long run, Taiwan will never be entirely safe from the mainland, but still may play a historical role in China. Taiwan may even provide future leaders for China.

MR. MYERS: Taiwan is developing a very strong position and is becoming attractive to much of China. This development presents many possibilities that were not there as recently as two or three years ago.

The independence issue is a difficult one. I agree with Professor Leng that the resolution should come over a period of time from Taiwan's strength and negotiation with Beijing.

I think Professor Leng's observation in regard to Philippines is correct. It is an interesting arrangement to have a fairly efficient and flourishing democracy within an oligarchical society. Power, money, and leadership in the Philippines are concentrated among perhaps a hundred families. You tend to throw out the rascals and end up with another group of rascals.

There are many people surrounding Mrs. Aquino from her family. Marcos's supporters claim that there is more corruption now than there was under Marcos, but that is hard to believe. Mrs. Aquino is probably the largest landowner in the Philippines, but nonetheless she has tried to promote official government channels rather than have everything come through the palace. This is a step in the right direction.

Economic growth in the Philippines stands at roughly 5 percent—not bad considering the difficulties. The Philippines is cursed with the oligarchical system, more the fault of the Spaniards than the Americans. Still, Americans have their fair share of guilt. During the long period of United States occupation, we were indiscriminate in our business partners. We pay for that legacy, as do the Filipinos.

I would like to make a couple of observations about American democracy. For a great majority of us, American democracy works fine, and maybe that is all we can expect. But Asia carefully follows the difficulties of American democracy.

The status quo in the United States suits an awful lot of people. Professor Hans Morgenthau, in grappling with American politics, said, I think it was in 1962, that the two great problems facing American democracy are racism and unemployment. These are the kinds of things that appear in the Asian press and are used to support either authoritarian solutions along the lines of Lee Kuan Yew or some kind of a redistributionist scheme that claims to eliminate problems of discrimination and poverty.

This summer Kurt Furgler, the former president of Switzerland, was in New York on the occasion of the 700th anniversary of the Swiss Confederation. In a rather moving speech he said that a democracy is judged by how it treats the least advantaged of its citizens. I think that to the extent that we effectively address these problems, we honor our concept of pluralism and provide a few standards of performance.

This is particularly true in the educational system. Some of you may have read Arthur M. Schlesinger's recent book, *The Disuniting of America*, in which he laments the loss of the melting pot idea and concern for the whole in America to the perpetuation and glorification of ethnicity.

All of those problems have a bearing on whether the Asian democracies succeed. If we do a poor job of American democracy, Asia will not find it worth emulating. Around the world recently, democracy has gone through a certain amount of triumphalism. It may be premature to say so, but democracy seems to have become the ethical standard for government.

Professor Morgenthau once said that where nothing is defined, nothing can be decided. His concern was rather prophetic: What might happen to the United States absent an external threat? Whether we are absent an external threat will be something people will debate, but Morgenthau thought that to the extent there was no external threat, American politics would likely be undefined, undecided, and issueless. Whether we are heading in that direction, you can judge.

QUESTION: Is the transfer of capital from Hong Kong to places such as Singapore, Malaysia, and Taiwan going to continue to build up those economies, or will this investment taper off?

MR. MYERS: My view is that anyone who is living in Hong Kong and has any money should get out. After 1997, when the PRC takes over, it will be not a happy place to live.

I was in Beijing about three years ago at a conference entitled "China in the World in the '90s," sponsored by the United Nations Development Program and the Ford Foundation. One of the people who attended was Lord Barber, who had been on the original committee that signed the Hong Kong agreement. Together we had an audience—I guess that is the right word—in the Great Hall of the People with Deng Xiaoping. What we didn't know was that the previous evening (this was in June 1988), there had been a small student demonstration in Beijing. Deng was quite agitated, and when the question of Hong Kong came up, he said that capitalism in Hong Kong would continue for at least 50 years as called for in the agreement. Then he said—this is why we were a little surprised—"But if any political trouble comes out of Hong Kong, I won't have it!" And he banged his fist! Lord Barber was shaken, because this was a clear indication that if there were political problems, the Chinese would not abide by the agreement, which is probably true. They are already interfering in arrangements regarding the elected legislature. I see nothing but bad news for people in Hong Kong, and over time, the function that Hong Kong has fulfilled will be transferred to Shanghai and other traditional financial places. Hong Kong will become more of a minor tourist stop, because it won't have any competitive advantage in manufacturing, for example, compared to southern China, and so on. Once this agreement is in place, many of the reasons Hong Kong has flourished will simply disappear.

QUESTION: We have recently seen the American military successfully deployed abroad in defense of Kuwait. At the same time, it now seems that the Senate of the Philippines will not renew the agreement on U.S. bases in that country. Have these developments affected what China might do militarily in the event that Taiwan declares independence or tries to enter the world arena more actively?

MR. MYERS: I think that the possibility of the mainland attacking Taiwan is something close to zero, because an attack on Taiwan would be like the old NATO scenario in Europe—in effect destroying the stake. We no longer have a defense treaty with Taiwan, but I think the possibility of going to war with China is a remote one.

QUESTION: I would like to explore your concerns about democracy in America. I was particularly attracted by your observation that the concept of the melting pot is being replaced by ethnic nationalism. Do you envision that this will put more pressure on the United States governance process toward a parliamentary system rather than a system in which a minority party can hold the chief executive office?

MR. MYERS: I believe in Los Angeles now there are something like 16 candidates for mayor based on various ethnic groups. If this trend continues with people insisting on representatives from their own ethnic group, the attractiveness of a parliamentary system is obvious. However, I don't see that happening in the foreseeable future.

We are working on a project at Tashkent State University in Uzbekistan. Tashkent is reminiscent of New York City: It has a population of about two million, comprising over 100 nationalities and a dozen religions. Under the Soviet system, which in effect enforced the concept of a melting pot, all of these people got along reasonably well. Without the lid, weaker ethnic groups are losing out to stronger ones. For example, the Koreans came to Tashkent in the 1930s, part of Stalin's resettlement program. Now the dominant groups in Tashkent want to send the Koreans back to Siberia and take over their property.

When these things get out of hand, it is hard to predict the ultimate course. If you can't come up with some meaningful transcendental ideas, nationalism degenerates into separatism, which could be disastrous for the United States and elsewhere.

QUESTION: You mentioned the problem of the multiplicity of political parties in Korea. Haven't we had a long-standing historical example of that in France between World Wars I and II? It was disorderly and you might say it didn't work very well, but no one talked about changing the French system.

MR. MYERS: In France they have a president and a cabinet system that allows majorities. The problem in Korea and in the Philippines is that under a presidential system, you are likely to have a minority government. With a cabinet system, a minority government can put together coalitions as they do in Italy, where a new coalition, fashioned every six months and receiving 51 percent of the vote, forms a new government.

This is the problem to which I refer. It doesn't bother me as much as it bothers the Koreans. They don't want to face a situation where the government does not hold a majority in the national assembly, and one way to avoid that is to have a cabinet system rather than a presidential system.

NARRATOR: About 20 years ago, Professor O. D. Corpus from the University of the Philippines wrote a piece called "The Two Faces of Philippine Morality," which addressed the problems of then President Carlos Garcia. Garcia had been challenged by the legislature for using the palace to funnel money to his relatives. Professor Corpus's conclusion was that in the Philippines there are two areas of morality: one toward the state and the other to your family. If the two come into conflict, the morality of the family takes precedence. This is one of the challenges we face in Asia that makes Dr. Myers' work so worthwhile. We thank Dr. Myers very much, and we thank Professors Lin and Leng.

CHAPTER TWO

Current International Trends and the two Koreas*

HAKJOON KIM

This chapter is an attempt to review the current trends in international politics in general and in the Asia-Pacific region in particular.

I

Currently popular among western scholars is a rediscovered classic, *History of the Peloponnesian War* by Thucydides.[1] Detailed in this work is the history of how the democratic Athenian system finally succeeded in annihilating Sparta armed with its rigid dictatorial system. The reason for the current revival of interest in the book is that it offers a definite lesson concerning what occurred in recent world history: collapse of the former Soviet Union symbolizing the totalitarian dictatorship and the rise of the Western democratic systems. In this context, Samuel P. Huntington writes

Hakjoon Kim, a professor of political science at Dankook University in Seoul, Korea, received his Ph.D. from the University of Pittsburgh in 1972. He was a member of the 12th National Assembly of South Korea and chief press secretary to and spokesperson for the South Korean president. He is the recipient of the 1983 Best Book Prize awarded by the Korean Political Science Association. His publications in English include Korea's Relations with Her Neighbours in a Changing World *(Elizabeth, N.J.: Hollym International Corporation, 1993).*

that "today we are going through a phase not of deepening pessimism but of triumphant euphoria about democracy. People speak of the global democratic revolution and the end of history."[2]

As recently as two decades ago, there were those among Western scholars who tended to predict the decline of the democratic countries of the West. At that time, pessimism about the viability of the major democracies of Europe, North America, and Asia was widespread. Politicians, columnists, and scholars were asking with increasing frequency whether democracy was "in crisis." *The Crisis of Democracy*[3] reflected this tendency.

Since the late 1980s, pessimism rapidly grew. Paul Kennedy's monumental work[4] contributed to the rise of this trend, which was known among academics as "declinism." According to him, the United States, like the powerful nations that have gone before it, is caught on the horns of dilemma. The wealth and economic development of the United States is being challenged and may someday be eclipsed by the other major powers.

The "declinists" also stressed the darker side of Western democratic societies. The Western world's collection of inveterate evils—for example, violence, drugs, sexual/moral problems, the widening gap between the rich and poor, and the collapse of the traditional family structure—were all threatening the Western democratic system. Warnings were being sounded that as a result, Western democratic governments were facing a crisis in which they were gradually losing even the "ability to govern." On the other hand, it was commonly believed that Communist dictatorships and the authoritarian systems of third world countries, while they might be subject to endless challenges to their legitimacy, would be able to continue their respective systems by strengthening their effectiveness.

However, actual history has shown the exact opposite to be true. In the last few years it has become obvious that, first in the field of international politics, the United States exercises the single firmest hegemony. Indeed, American democracy has demonstrated a capacity for resilience and rejuvenation.[5] The threats posed by the Soviet Union and by Western European Communist parties have all but disappeared. As a result, it is widely accepted that the present period is characterized by the preponderance of American power[6] and that this era will continue for at least the next decade or so.

In addition, Western Europe is nowhere near to being on the path to decline. While there have been some twists and turns in the road, thus sometimes reviving a new wave of Euro-pessimism, this area of the world is heading down the path of peace and prosperity. It is evidenced in the formal inauguration of the European Union in November 1993 and of the European Economic Area (EEA) in January 1994.

European unity will not remain at that level, however. The Europeans are headed in the direction of a complete system of political unity or what we might describe as "the United States of Europe." In the process, starting with Russia and followed by the nations of Eastern Europe, affiliation and cooperation in certain areas has already been initiated. Some Western European members of NATO, particularly Germany, have even attempted to expand its membership into the Eastern European countries. Meanwhile, the North Atlantic Cooperation Council (NACC), an adjunct to the alliance, provides a framework within which NATO countries are developing a wide array of cooperative ties to former Warsaw Pact and former Soviet states.[7] Against the backdrop of the potential powder keg in Southeastern and Eastern Europe, however, NATO's relevance to post-Cold War security planning lies in its ongoing ability to keep the United States tied to European security planning.[8] Of course, the United States will continue to maintain a joint security and cooperative system with the European Union more broadly and NATO specifically.

In a word, Pax Americana or the era of American-led peace in North America and Western Europe denotes a state of security that will continue into the foreseeable future. Indeed, in terms of major security challenges, Western democracies are now more secure than at any time since Hitler came to power.[9] Thus, one may denounce defeatism and deplore any thought of decline.

In the realm of international economics, we will see a somewhat different scenario being played out, however. The world economy will move from the age of protectionism and cliquism to regionalism. The United States will not be able to lead the world in this area. It will have to be satisfied with the decentralization of its control of the world's economy. In turn, we will face the prospects of a merciless economic war between regions or trade blocs.

To elaborate on this, from the perspective of international economics, the world will be divided into three trade blocs. These are the European Economic Area, the North American Free Trade Agreement (NAFTA), and the "Asia-Pacific sphere" as symbolized by the Asian-Pacific Economic Coordination (APEC) organization, although it "is a purely consultative forum."[10] In Europe, Germany and France will exercise control; in Asia, China and Japan will emerge as leaders; and in North America, the United States will retain control while at the same time exerting a tremendous amount of influence on the remaining two areas. Already this has become very pronounced in the launching of the World Trade Organization (WTO) in 1994. In the future, the world economy will be a hotbed of unrestricted competition and conflict between the developed countries of the West and the East. Thus, the future portends a trade and economic war.

Until now, this essay has surveyed trends in the West's international politics and economics. Now let us turn our attention to what the domestic situations of these countries will be. I have already suggested in this essay that the West is on the road to prosperity. What is it, then, that has led the West onto this road? That answer was suggested by our reading of *History of the Peloponnesian War* and is nothing more than what may be described as the "spirit" of a people. A system or a polity that stimulates the spirit of a people must lead to a prosperous nation. A repressive system or polity makes for the decline of a nation. What is described as being something that encourages the vitality of a people is, in political terms, also describing a democratic system that respects the freedom of the individual and human rights. In economic terms it is a capitalist system that values the principles of a market economy and the pursuit of individual profit. In the realm of social culture it is a spirit that is both unregulated, creative, and contributes to the growth of value systems and diversity. The heart of a democratic society is competition with good intentions—one that encourages and protects the development of a healthy competitive culture. In the future, therefore, this type of competition must not be thought as criminal, nor must it be allowed to weaken. Much creativity arises as a result of bona fide competition.

Recently, the rather idealized view of government as providing all of the benefits of a welfare state has come under criticism. The results of this phenomenon have given us little new learning. In countries where governments in the name of social security provide many benefits, the culture of capitalism has weakened, and man's creative spirit and motivation to achieve has lessened. People covet ease and a multitude of other problems: drugs, sexual license, and the breakdown of the social order all follow. In this context, observations of Michel Crozier, the founder and president of the Centre for Organizational Sociology in Paris, merit lengthy quotation:

> In the 1970s, Sweden was still regarded as a model of enlightened public management. It is now undergoing such a crisis that its social democratic approach cannot be considered a model at all. Its welfare system appears not only so costly that the country cannot afford it in its present economic circumstances, but also too bureaucratic to give its citizens the minimum satisfaction they expect. Individualism, meanwhile, is undermining the traditional discipline that kept the system going. Tax evasion, if not outright corruption, is spreading, while commitment declines and productivity stagnates.[11]

But with these words, I do no mean to raise competitive culture to the level of a new god. Healthy competition should be encouraged, but within the bounds of just law, system, and customary practice.

In summary, the United States, Western Europe, and the rest of the world through the continued development of free democracy are going through an era of "Democratic Renaissance." It is evidenced that "since the 1970s, the global tide in regime transformations has been not against democracy but overwhelmingly in its favor. In the past 20 years, about 40 countries have shifted from authoritarianism to democratic rule."[12]

To be more specific, first in light of the collapse of the confrontational structure of the Cold War and in turn the weakening of the military, new civilian democratic political leadership continues to become stronger. "By and large these new democratic regimes have been reasonably successful in establishing civilian control, in orienting their militaries toward professionalism, in reducing military power, in constricting military roles, and in establishing patterns of civil-military relationship that resemble those in established democracies."[13]

Second, the restrictive bureaucracy that hampered development in previous generations has been relaxed. Indeed, "what is slowing progress is not the citizenry or opposition to collective action, but entrenched bureaucratic systems that are interconnected with political parties, the government, and to some extent, the business establishment."[14] The present Italian crisis, and to a lesser extent the Japanese crisis, provides excellent examples. However, "a clash between a changed citizenry and a backward state unable to act in acceptable moral terms is bringing fundamental change."[15] In France, too, "there is a new questioning of organizational structures and a new effort to professionalize people, suppress hierarchies, and simplify procedures."[16]

Third, the framework for the administration of programs for the welfare of citizens is being simplified. "The more bureaucratic a system becomes, the more likely it is that the human qualities so important to helping the underprivileged will disappear."[17] In this context, the new trend to reduce complexity is most welcomed. Fourth, autonomous regional governments have been strengthened.

All of these steps have led to a leap in vitality and creativity on the part of the citizenry. More than anything else, the most significant thing has been that the role of citizens has been enlarged. Among most Western democracies, citizens are ahead of their institutions. In turn, this means that the consciousness and behavior of citizens themselves should be more improved quality-wise.

To bolster the trend for "Democratic Renaissance," capitalistic economic growth and development should be accompanied. In the event that the economy does not operate effectively, then democratic development in that country also becomes difficult.

Hakjoon Kim

In order to increase international competitiveness and for the development of capitalist-style economics, developed countries in the West and developing countries must boldly pursue their own economic reform. If they are going to prosper economically and compete globally, major economic liberalization is necessary. They need to open their markets and remove subsidies and restrictive regulations. The vicious linkage between political power and economic power, which symbolizes "a backward but very weak state and a corrupt political system,"[18] should be dissolved. Corrupt government officials must be fired.

If democracy and economic development continue to develop together, it is the sense of many intellectuals that beginning with domestic prosperity, this will spread to stability and peace. Indeed, the recent history of many countries have shown that economic growth, political democratization, and peace constitute a virtuous cycle. Peace and stability are necessary (though not sufficient) conditions for rapid economic growth in many developing countries. Economic development has created middle classes that have accelerated an end to authoritarian rule. Strengthening democratic regimes have led to more stable and peaceful relations among nations. The forces of the "growth-democracy-peace triangle"[19] have tended to work jointly to promote a more peaceful and stable regional order. Accordingly, maintaining this economic development presupposes the peace and stability that made it possible.[20]

In sum, Western democratic countries and most developing countries are doing their best to form the permanent structure of the "growth-democracy-peace triangle." In addition, sociologically, the major premise is the rapid recovery of moral health. The success or failure of this will be the major factor in determining the future of the Western world.

II

In the previous section, I argued that the future of the Western world appears to be comparatively good. Many experts on world affairs go on to posit a type of "the triumphalist expectation" or "triumphalism."[21] Much like 1919 and 1945, the dominant mood at the end of the Cold War was the triumphalist expectation that the values which had won the war would now produce the expansion of democracy. The belief was that if a democratic system was disseminated throughout the world, then international peace could be maintained.

But triumphalism always has a short life. After the First World War, militaristic dictatorship became rampant and eventually sparked a new world war. In addition, after the Second World War, an unyielding spirit of totalitarian dictatorship emerged and enveloped the world in an ideological Cold War and at times even plunged it into active war. After the end of the Cold war, as before, "triumphalism gave way to disillusionment and disorientation, both in the United States and in Europe, as these sanguine expectations inevitably were shattered."[22]

The main rational for this is based upon the development of a political situation in the former "Soviet Empire." By the former "Soviet Empire," I mean, of course, the now defunct Soviet Union and the Eastern European countries that fell under the Soviet sphere of influence. Imagine if the former Soviet Union itself or the Russian Federation or even the Eastern European countries were to go through a new series of violent upheavals and end up in a state of reactionism. The comparatively optimistic future predicted in the previous section would then be subject to a tremendous shock. In that vein, let us in this section examine what the future direction of the former "Soviet Empire" will be.

To begin, let us first attempt to diagnose what Russia's actual state is today. Particularly since the breakup of the Soviet Union in 1991, the process for the dismantling of communism has been underway. At the initial stage, the reform-oriented leaders assessed that "Russia is already a different society where there is no place for the reactionary forces."[23] Their assessment has proved to be too optimistic, however.

In December 1993, for the first time following the Bolshevik Revolution of 1917, free elections were held in the Russian Federation. As the results of this election tell us, the hope that surrounded the new Russian style of political reform and openness was dealt a severe blow. These results showed that "half of Russia chooses totalitarians."[24] In them, we may find a reemergence of

28

Russia's traditional tendency toward authoritarianism—just in a new form.

The fact that the anti-reform reactionary faction led by the extreme right-wing Russian nationalist Vladimir Zhirinovsky ended up finishing so strongly by getting 24 percent of the popular vote in the nationwide party voting is evidence of the growing sense of disappointment and frustration of the Russian people. In a word, Zhirinovsky, the man responsible for causing this "political earthquake" in Russian politics, is a Russian-style Hitler. He is both a radical racist and a fascist who advocates violence. He would even use force if necessary to rebuild the Soviet bloc and create a restored "Soviet Empire." He promised in his election campaign that he would even take back Alaska from the United States.[25]

The Russian people's sense of disappointment and feelings of frustration stem from the fact that the lack of consumer goods from which they suffered under the Communist regime has not been immediately rectified by the promises of capitalistic market economy principles. From the point of view of not only developed countries but also of newly industrializing countries such as South Korea, the situation that the people of Russia face is poor. Russia's almost fatal inflation rate and the lack of consumer goods have meant that her people have suffered tremendously. Added to this is the rapid increase in the disparity between the rich and poor. We are witnessing the appearance of a Russian version of the Weimar Republic.[26]

It is hardly necessary to mention that public peace and security can no longer be guaranteed. In 1992 the annual number of murders per 100,000 people stood at 16–17. Lebanon, a country in a state of civil war, has nearly the same number of murders. The *Moscow Times*, an English daily, in its 2 December 1993 edition deplored the fact that this statistic makes Russia the second most violent country in the world and gives clear evidence of the lack of public peace and security. Here, the combination of misgovernment, corruption, and disinterest on the part of government officials has meant that the ardent support the reform group enjoyed in the past has been greatly diminished.[27]

On the other hand, the constitution that was approved last December gave to President Yeltsin significant additional power, while at the same time greatly reducing the strength of the Duma, the Russian version of the British lower house. Therefore, Yeltsen and his reform group will not face major institutional obstacles to the execution of his pro-Western democratic and capitalist policies.

However, the problem is that the sociological climate of the country and the psychological attitude of the people have changed. The people no longer have respect for or any expectations about political reform. It is evidenced in the fact that nowadays former Soviet President Gorbachev has fallen from the position of highly respected leader to that of an unpopular politician. Russia's current President Yeltsin, who with his firm opposition to a reactionary coup d'etat of 1991 became a democratic hero, is today the object of disappointment and even severe criticism. There are many who speculate publicly on the probabilities of Yeltsin remaining in office long enough to complete his term in 1996. If they now place their hopes for the future in a reactionist, anti-Western, and chauvinistic Russia, this will not only darken the future of Russia but will also intensify friction and discord with the West.

Another factor that adds to our worries about Russia's future is specifically the Islamic countries. Originally, these countries were part of the Soviet Union and now they have become independent. Among these countries are those that are greatly influenced by Islamic fundamentalism, which aggressively challenges world order and Western civilization. These countries are already thought of as being dangerous entities not only in their relations with Russia, but also with Europe and the pro-Western countries of the Middle East.

Eastern Europe is not in as serious a situation. In the fall of 1989, when the Berlin Wall fell, the people of Eastern Europe cried, as if in one voice, "for democracy, markets and the West—from the Baltic to the Balkans." Their cry for the West was a cry not only for integration with a prosperous, secure West but also replication of Western Europe's postwar success in overcoming destructive nationalism.[28] These people were filled with brand new hope.

From the three nations of the Baltic to Albania, all Eastern European countries no longer wanted to be thought of as being former "Eastern" European Communist countries. Rather, they insisted that they be included as a part of Western Europe. They rejected even the term *Eastern* Europe itself as being tainted and cursed, a suggestion of their former chains to the Soviet Union. They believed that they could operate Western-style democracies and that through their choice of market economies, they themselves could improve their human condition. In sum, the abrupt collapse of Communist regimes throughout Eastern Europe during the last months of 1989 created widespread hope for a comparatively rapid transition to political democracy and market economies.

In the space of a few brief years, however, the terms *privatization* and *capitalism* became the targets of a new type of hatred. As was true in Russia, the difference between rich and poor has steadily widened. The newly rich were generally those who in the past had good positions in either the Communist party, government, or government-operated industries. The average citizen had ample reason to distrust the government. To put it simply, theirs was a deep suspicion that when the Communist system collapsed, the public funds and materials of the party, government, and state industries would be snatched away. These one-time flunkies just switched hats and became businessmen.

As a result of this disappointment and distrust, Eastern European intellectuals even thought of creating a "Marxism Without Russia" or a "Social Egalitarianism Without Guns or Swords of Totalitarianism." The people, however, were looking for a scapegoat on whom to pin their hatred and despair about the future. This took the form it was taking in Russia: radical racism, nationalism, religious intolerance, fascism, and anti-Semitism.

In the former Yugoslav Federation, the shedding of blood accompanied dissolution and a fearful civil war. In particular, the continuation of Bosnia's bloody civil war speaks eloquently of how greatly one situation in Eastern Europe can affect world harmony and cooperation. If this conflict is not contained and spreads to involve Russia and surrounding countries, it will become an explosive device within the former Soviet Empire. If it explodes, it will threaten the general security and peace of the Western world.

The Western world is well aware of the consequences of problems within the former Soviet Empire, thus it is doing its utmost to aid the Yeltsin government and support the transition of Eastern Europe from communism to postcommunism. In certain areas we are seeing results.

In the midst of the widening of the Yeltsin administration's efforts at privatization, the government has been successful to a certain extent in laying the foundations for promoting an ambitious economic reform policy. In Poland, flourishing private enterprise now accounts for over one-half of the country's domestic gross national product. Hungary's trade with the West has increased greatly. The countries of the Czech Republic and Slovakia with their positive strategy toward privatization have excited the interest of Western investors. In the Balkan countries of Bulgaria, Romania, and Albania, however, results are yet to be as pronounced. In this context, one observer reports that "overall, what we are likely to witness is an 'Eastern Europe of multiple speed,' with some countries, like the Czech Republic and Slovakia, making the transition relatively smoothly and others, like Romania and Bulgaria, having much more difficulty and taking longer."[29]

Will the former Soviet Empire succeed in pro-Western democratic capitalistic reform? Or will it, as Czech President Vaclav Havel worries, turn into the "nightmare of [the] post-Communist world" and the revival of "authoritarianism and extremism"? From our point of view, success must first come through the efforts of the former Soviet Empire in their democratization process. Then, led by economic development and peace, the virtuous triangular cycle can be formed. As a result, political theory, which holds the Western world and its democratic values as fundamental, will become common property. On this foundation we can only pray that the roots of "perpetual world peace" can take hold.

We must acknowledge, however, that there is a limit to how much support the Western world can give to maintaining policies along those lines. Already we can discern the hints that the West is wary of extremely aggressive nationalistic cliques. In the end, we can only hope that the former Soviet Empire, through the development of a healthy competitive culture in which the spirit of the people is again awakened, will be able to follow the normal course of history. We pray that the transition of the former Soviet Empire into a stable democracy and a growing market economy will in the end be successfully concluded. There is one thing that is for certain. Depending on which final terminal this uncertain transition period brings the former Soviet Empire, it is a fact that the world's future in the 21st century will be subject to many changes.[30]

III

"If the Mediterranean Sea was the ocean of the past and if we call the Atlantic Ocean the ocean of today, then the Pacific Ocean will be the ocean of the future." If this prediction by then U.S. Secretary of State John Hay is right on the mark and if the Asia-Pacific region has developed to become the world's most dynamic economic region, then the region now truly holds the position of a new international political and economic axis. In particular, the Asia-Pacific region accounts for 44 percent of total world output and enjoys the highest rate of growth as well. Moreover, the amount of trade that now crosses across the Pacific has already surpassed the amount of trade that crossed the Atlantic in 1983. In addition, approximately 33 percent of the world's economic activity occurs in the Pacific[31] and the policy demands of the developed world toward the region have even overlapped to the extent that the first summit conference of APEC was held in November 1993 at Seattle.

In this particular climate, through the usual media channels the impression given to the average people about this region is that security and peace are close at hand. Indeed, the atmosphere of cooperation and harmony that has manifest itself after the end of the Cold War certainly includes this region that once had been severely affected by a variety of civil disturbances and wars. Therefore, it is easy for people to get the impression that this region, as its name implies—"The Ocean of Great Peace"—is truly peaceful.

That optimistic impression, when looked at in the larger sense, is not incorrect. It is certain that in this region also, for example, following the dismantling of the former Soviet Union, that the once huge Soviet Far Eastern military has been greatly reduced and that the chances for military confrontation between the Soviets (Russia) and the United States has in a similar fashion lessened. Even China and Russia, who at one point had gone to the brink of war, have normalized their relations. In Indochina, in 1993, the Cambodian civil war was resolved and now expectations of peace bring a new aspect of hope to life there. In the Middle East there are also isolated instances of reconciliation. In sum, in the Asia-Pacific region there are affirmative applications of a definite security process. South Korea has established diplomatic relations with the Soviet Union in 1990 and the People's Republic of China in 1992. The emperor of Japan visited China in 1992 and the psychological adjustment between the two countries can be viewed as successfully resolved. In a word, the ideological conflict that characterized the Asia-Pacific region and the zero-sum game of brinkmanship has generally become a thing of the past.

Along the same lines, we must regard the nations of this region on the basis of pragmatism and rationality. If we do so, then we are able to confirm that strength has been gathered from democratization and economic development. National strength, once concentrated on external military confrontation, is now starting to concentrate on democratization, economic development, and peace—the triangular virtuous cycle. We can discover similar progress in many nations.

We have a comparatively optimistic attitude about the formation of the triangular virtuous cycle in the Asia-Pacific region. Among the reasons for this, the most important is that in the major nations of this region the previous generation's authoritarian systems and its leaders have either fallen or been forced from office. With the appearance of civilian reform and rational leaders, civil servants are moving forward in preparation for the 21st century. When we consider the various elements that make up the Asia-Pacific region on the brink of the 21st century, it is not unrealistic to think of inaugurating a cooperative security organization that is basically similar to that of Europe's CSCE (Conference on Security and Cooperation in Europe). In contemporary Asia, there is unlikely to be an effective Conference on Security and Cooperation in Asia (CSCA) comprising all Asian countries, as proposed by the former Soviet Union and Australia.[32] If we are able to inaugurate an organization such as this, however, we will be able to raise the level of security and peace in this region to a high level.

On the other hand, it would also be wise to turn our eyes to the fact that the future of the Asia-Pacific region is not all that rosy. One evidence of this fact comes from the conflict between Japan and Russia over the northern territories, an issue that has lingered unresolved since the end of World War II. It is hardly necessary to mention the continuation of the division of the Korean Peninsula and the conflict between North and South.

Evidence that ideological conflicts remain can be found in the fact that some countries have not abandoned communism. In the case of North Korea, it is the world's most confrontational and closed Communist system. They are also making efforts (which have proved futile) to export the militant *Juche* (self-reliance) ideology or Kim-Il-Sungism to other regions as well.

More than these factors, there are other aspects that demand analysis; that is, the tendency toward the augmentation of military strength. While in fact the international Cold War has ended, expenditures for military items have continued to rise in the Asia-Pacific region. The overarming of states in the region is more strikingly reflected in the list of leading importers of major conventional weapons for 1986 to 1990. As Hee-Kwon Park has indicated, of the 15 top importers, 14 countries except one (Angola) is located in Asia and the Middle East. Moreover, these 14 countries accounted for 75 percent of all major conventional weapons imports in the developing world during the same period. The most noticeable characteristics of conventional arms imports in the region is that Asia-Pacific countries have begun to diversify with regard to their conventional weapons suppliers. Unlike the Cold War period, when the United States was the major arms supplier to regional countries, a number of Asian countries—China, Malaysia, Indonesia, Taiwan, the Philippines, Burma, and Thailand—have shown strong interest in the arms exports of Russian and Eastern European countries.[33]

Why is it that in this era of post-Cold War rapprochement, this region is using a tremendous amount of its financial resources to augment its military power? The basic reason is the common belief among the Asia-Pacific countries that at some point in the future the struggle for regional hegemony between Japan and China will proceed to a point that becomes threatening to the entire region.

In looking at China's current domestic situation, we may pay attention to the fact that in the near future the country will have to deal with the death of Deng Xiaoping and a crisis of succession as well as a gradual increase in the regional decentralization of power. In fact, moves toward "*de facto* separation" have begun in certain coastal provinces. In this vein, Gerald Segal concludes that "what seems to be emerging now is a less tightly ruled China, and one that is being pulled in different directions by the outside world."[34] When these points are considered, one can predict that at least until the end of the 20th century, even though military expenditures may increase to a certain extent, they will not move in the direction of external expansionism.

Japan, of course, has already made her position clear. It wants to cut all ties to its militaristic and imperialistic pre-war stance. My evaluation is that the new Japanese leadership and its supporters are only interested in making Japan an "Economic and Political Superpower" and do not want to repeat the mistakes of "Imperialist Japan."

However, first with respect to China, as we move into the 21st century: China will become a fourth pole after the United States, Japan, and the European Union (particularly Germany). This is particularly true when one looks at "Greater China," consisting of the People's Republic, Hong Kong, and Taiwan. According to World Bank projections, Greater China's net imports in the year 2002 will be $639 billion, compared to $521 billion for Japan. Likewise, using comparable international prices, Greater China in the year 2002 is projected to have a gross domestic product of $9.8 trillion, compared to $9.7 trillion for the United States. As Nicholas D. Kristof has pointed out, if those forecasts hold, in other words, Greater China would not just be another economic pole; it would be the biggest of them all[35] and it will exercise greater independent political influence. If at this time, China does not cooperate with the West as led by the United States and instead allies itself with Muslim countries and adopts the posture of confronting the West, the peace and security of the Asia-Pacific region will face a serious challenge. Against this backdrop, we are compelled to pay serious attention to the recent increase in China's military expenditures.

On the one hand, Japan will be subject to the suspicion that they will "revive the unhappy history of the past" and face "the burden of continuity." If these suspicions cannot be kept suppressed, then countries in this region will not be able to get over their wariness of Japan. They will continuously be watching to see if Japan will become a nuclear power.

In this vein, a new argument advanced by the junior group of the Japanese Ministry of Foreign Affairs has received serious attention from Japan's Asian neighbors. It was the "Leave USA; Enter Asia" theory, a reversal of the theory first proposed by Fukujawa Yukichi immediately after the Meiji Restoration, which was the "Leave Asia; Enter Europe" theory. The new argument insists that the Japanese should leave the United States's sphere of influence and enter into Asia's. In my analysis, that is fundamentally a pro-Asia theory, but it is attracting in general serious concern from Asians.[36]

ENDNOTES

1. For example, see Paul A. Rahe, "Justice, Necessity, and the Conduct of War in Thucydides," a paper read at the Woodrow Wilson International Center for Scholars, Washington, D.C., on 25 January 1994; and Laurie M. Johnson Bagby, "The Use and Abuse of Thucydides in International Relations," *International Organization*, vol. 48, no. 1 (Winter 1994), 131-153.

2. Samuel P. Huntington, "The Ungovernability of Democracy," *The American Enterprise*, vol. 4, no. 6 (November-December 1993), 35.

3. Samuel P. Huntington, Michel Crozier, and Joji Watanuki, *The Crisis of Democracy* (New York: New York University Press, 1975). This book was the result of a report submitted to the Trilateral Commission directed by Zbigniew Brzezinski.

4. Paul Kennedy, *The Rise and Fall of the Great Powers: Economic Change and Military Conflict from 1500 to 2000* (New York: Random House, 1987).

5. Kenneth W. Thompson, *Traditions and Values in Politics and Diplomacy: Theory and Practice* (Baton Rouge: Louisiana State University Press, 1992), 309.

6. Charles Krauthammer, "The Unipolar Moment," *Foreign Affairs*, vol. 70, no. 1 (1990-91), 23–33; Melvyn P. Leffler, *A Preponderance of Power: National Security, the Truman Administration, and the Cold War* (Stanford: Stanford University Press, 1992); and for the criticism of these arguments, see Christopher Layne, "The Unipolar Illusion: Why New Great Powers will Rise," *International Security*, vol. 17, no. 4 (Spring 1993), 5–51.

7. Stanley R. Sloan, "Global Burdensharing in the Post–Cold War World," *CRS Report for Congress* (Washington, D.C.:

Congressional Research Service, The Library of Congress, 8 October 1993), 38.

8. Jacquelyn Davis, "Restructuring of Military Force in Europe," a paper read at the IISS 35th Annual Conference held at Brussels on 9–12 September 1993, 3.

9. Huntington, "The Ungovernability of Democracy," 35.

10. Frank B. Gibney, "Creating a Pacific Community: A Time to Bolster Economic Institutions," *Foreign Affairs*, vol. 72, no. 5 (November-December 1993), 21.

11. Michel Crozier, "The Ungovernability of Democracy," *The American Enterprise*, vol. 4, no. 6 (November-December 1993), 29.

12. Huntington, "The Ungovernability of Democracy," 35.

13. Ibid., 36.

14. Crozier, "The Ungovernability of Democracy," 30.

15. Ibid.

16. Ibid.

17. Ibid., 33.

18. Ibid., 30.

19. Steve Chan, "National Security in the Asia-Pacific: Linkages Among Growth, Democracy and Peace," *Contemporary Southeast Asia*, vol. 14, no. 1 (June 1992), 18–25.

20. Hee-kwon Park, "Multilateral Security Cooperation," *The Pacific Review*, vol. 6, no. 3 (1993), 262.

21. Robert L. Hutchings, "Beyond the Cold War: American Diplomacy, 1989 and After," a paper read at the Woodrow Wilson International Center for Scholars, Washington, D.C., on 5 November 1993, 16 and 27.

22. Ibid., 27.

23. Cited by Gilbert Rozman, "Stages in the Reform and Dismantling of Communism in China and the Soviet Union," in Gilbert Rozman (ed.), *Dismantling Communism: Common Causes and Regional Variations* (Washington, D.C.: The Woodrow Wilson Center Press, 1992), 17.

24. Charles Krauthammer, "Russian Earthquake: The Meaning of Zhirinovsky," *Washington Post*, 17 December 1993.

25. Ibid.

26. I visited Moscow and St. Petersburg just before the elections and met a good number of intellectuals. See my "Dialogues with Russian and Eastern European Intellectuals [in Korean]," *Oekyo* [Seoul: "Diplomacy," a quarterly], no. 29 (March 1994), 126–130. See also my "Professor Hakjoon Kim's Visit to Russia [in Korean]," *Shindong'a* [Seoul: "New East Asia," a monthly] (February 1992), 622–631.

27. Celestine Bohlen, "Graft and Gangsterism in Russia Blight the Entrepreneurial Spirit," *New York Times*, 30 January 1994.

28. Hutchings, "Beyond the Cold War," 17. See also John R. Lampe (ed.), *Creating Capital Markets in Eastern Europe* (Washington, D.C.: The Woodrow Wilson International Center for Scholars, 1992).

29. F. Stephen Larrabee, "Democratization and Change in Eastern Europe," in Samuel F. Wells, Jr. (ed.), *The Helsinki Process and the Future of Europe* (Washington, D.C.: The Woodrow Wilson Center Press, 1990), 41.

30. For cautious optimism in this regard, see Vladimir I. Ivanov, "Japan, Russia, and the United States: Prospects for Cooperative Relations in the New Era," a conference report prepared in July 1993 and distributed by the United States Institute of Peace, Washington, D.C.

31. In 1991, United States trade with Asia-Pacific nations reached $300 billion, three times more than America's trade with Latin America and 50 percent more than its trade with Western Europe. Park, "Multilateral Security Cooperation," 262.

32. Ibid., 252.

33. Ibid., 258-259.

34. Gerald Segal, "China Changes Shape: Regionalism and Foreign Policy," *Adelphi Papers* no. 287 (London: The International Institute for Strategic Studies, 1994), 3.

35. Nicholas D. Kristof, "The Rise of China," *Foreign Affairs*, vol. 72, no. 5 (November-December 1993), 61-62.

36. *Mainichi Shimbun* [Tokyo: "Daily Newspaper"], 13 November 1993.

CHAPTER THREE

Korea in a World of Change*

ROBERT J. MYERS

NARRATOR: Robert Myers is a scholar, an author, an adminis-trator, a former publisher of *The New Republic*, and co-founder and publisher of *Washingtonian* magazine. He served as vice president and director of the Liveright Publishing Company and vice president of New Republic Books. He has also had remarkable success as the president of the Carnegie Council on Ethics and International Affairs, raising the endowment of that organization from $4 or $5 million to $22 million.

Dr. Myers has been the editor for special issues of *Annals of the American Academy of Political and Social Sciences*. He has also written *The Coming Collapse of the Post Office* and has edited and written works on international politics and ethics, including the edited volume of *The Political Morality of the International Monetary Fund*. He is author of a summer 1992 article on "Roh Tae Woo and the Future of Korean Democracy"; he also is the author of "Rethinking Human Rights" in the November-December 1992 issue of *Society* magazine. He is currently working on a book on foreign policy.

Dr. Myers served in Korea in April and May of 1992, where he has had a long and intimate association with leaders, scholars, educators, and scientists.

Presented in a Forum at the Miller Center of Public Affairs on 29 May 1992.

MR. MYERS: My role today was supposed to have been to introduce Hyun Hong-Choo, who has been a cabinet officer in Korea in various capacities, including legislative minister and campaign manager, for what was then the Democratic Justice party of current South Korean President Roh Tae Woo. Hyun Hong-Choo is a fine speaker with many insights into the political scene in Korea. He had to return to Seoul, however, so I was invited to speak on the Korean scene in his place.

I have found over the years that a discussion about democracy in a single country, particularly one that has gone through the colonial period and then through the developmental stage, is enhanced by comparing its situation to other situations. Judging any country on only its own terms makes it difficult to get a feel for whether it is going forward or backward.

Korea's history goes back several thousand years, but from an international relations and foreign policy viewpoint, it dates from the end of World War II. The Japanese had taken over Korea in 1910 and subjected it to a particularly brutal colonial period. They were not content to simply occupy the country and seize its agricultural and minor industrial assets. They also tried to incorporate Korea into Japanese culture. The Koreans were forced to take Japanese names, and the Korean language was no longer taught in the schools. It was a period that is really quite hard to conceive in modern terms, particularly when one looks at British colonialism, as well as the United States colonial administration in the Philippines. Even though those administrations may have been very misguided and the results very mixed, it was not their intention to obliterate the culture of other countries. The Japanese, on the other hand, have much to answer for.

The Koreans went through three distinct periods after World War II. The first is what I would call the Nationalist period under Syngman Rhee. I had the privilege of witnessing the Korean independence movement in China. Three distinct Korean groups had tried to claim power when World War II ended. One was the group I was with in China under the Nationalist government led by Kim Koo. A second group was supported by the Soviets in Manchuria and led by Kim Il Sung. The third group was based in Hawaii and Washington under Syngman Rhee and his very

44

charming Austrian wife, who died this year. With the Americans finally occupying the South, it was not surprising that Syngman Rhee and the Methodist Church faction carried the day, and he became the country's first president in 1948. Kim Koo was later to be assassinated by the head of Syngman Rhee's police, and Kim Il Sung was to take over North Korea, where he remained until his death.

The second period began with the ouster of Syngman Rhee and his very brief successor, Chang Myon, in a coup by Park Chung Hee, who remained in power for approximately 20 years until he too was assassinated. That period of Korean history is usually called the "garrison state." As you remember, the war between North and South Korea wound up right back where it had begun, at the 38th parallel with no peace settlement. Both North and South Korea lived under a siege mentality, where national defense was the first priority, which led to a dampening of political activity and difficult internal security measures in the South.

It also led to enormous economic concentration and dedication, however. Park Chung Hee saw immediately that South Korea would get nowhere making shoes and textiles, so he began organizing the Korean industries through the *Chaebol* system, which is sort of like the Japanese *zaibatsu*. Under this system, the government poured money into big companies at very low, sometimes negative, interest rates. As a result, South Korea was a great place to be if you were interested in developing the country and making a lot of money for yourself.

Only recently have we seen that building up these enormous conglomerates was highly inefficient; most of them are awash in seas of debt. They are losing market share, and inflation in Korea is rising due to the fact that they can no longer export as they did, and everything is available on the local market quite cheaply. It is so cheap, as a matter of fact, that I have never seen such traffic jams in my life. The Koreans now have a system where helicopters lift disabled cars out of the middle of the 16-lane highways so that traffic flows uninterrupted.

Mainly good came of this in that South Korea has become an industrialized country. I have defined industrialization and modernization as taking place in four stages. The first is stability, which is an important part of the Confucian idea of a successful society. The trouble is that some people would be happy to leave it that way. It is the excuse of tyrants, that stability is to be the main end of life. The second stage is economic development, which by definition shakes up and changes everything. It is Schumpeter's notion of the "creative destruction" of capitalism: Everything is destroyed every day and comes back in a better way. The third stage is social participation in society, which involves voting and the formation of political parties. The final stage, which the South Koreans are now experiencing—as are we—still involves the notion of social justice: What is the good man; what is the good citizen; what is a good society?

With the assassination of Park Chung Hee in 1979, there was hope that the government would evolve into something with some democratic pretensions, but that was not to be. Another general, Chun Doo Hwan, seized power in a 1980 coup and basically continued the policies of Park Chung Hee in the economic field. He did little to enter into the third and fourth steps of development that I mentioned. There was little participation in the government by the general population and no particular notion of social justice or any of the other good things that I mentioned. Resentment against policy gradually rose. I am pleased to see that in other places in Asia, change has also come about. I was surprised earlier this year when Lee Kuan Yew, the former longtime prime minister of Singapore, conceded that after undergoing economic development and educating the population, it becomes impossible to successfully run an authoritarian government. Lee even promoted the idea in Singapore that at a certain stage an authoritarian government would not work. We will see if he meant what he said, because Singapore is experiencing an economic decline. Lee's party won less than 70 percent of the vote in 1991, and for him that is a real slap in the face. We will see what happens.

The issue then in Korea in 1987 at the end of Chun's seven-year presidential term was whether there could be some kind of transfer of power or whether the constitution would be manipulated once again to enable Chun to run again. Aristotle told us that if you have a constitutional government, you had better be careful about amending the constitution. That lesson has not yet been learned in Korea or China, where they have frequently amended their constitutions at the convenience of the powers that be.

The issue surrounding Roh Tae Woo, who was then the head of the ruling Democratic Justice party, briefly is this: The nomination process by political parties in Korea in some ways isn't much different from that of the United States, except that all of those doing the nominating are members of the national assembly. This pretty well guarantees that when the party says they want *A* to run, *A* will be the nominee. The protest raised against this system by the students—who rioted in the streets—was that the president should be directly elected by the people, and that the nomination process should be more popular.

On 27 June 1987, party nominee Roh Tae Woo called for direct elections. If the national assembly wouldn't agree to that, he would step down as the nominee. That seemingly simply move produced temporary miracles. Everyone thought that now they would at least have a real chance to express their preference and that their vote would mean something in the actual election. A few days later, President Chun Doo Hwan also supported that process, so the arrangement for a peaceful transfer of power finally seemed to be at hand.

Essentially two people ran against Roh, and that has something to do with today's situation as well. One was Kim Dae Jung, who has been somewhat of a hero. He has been harried by the government, arrested, and given a death sentence, but he has survived. The other was the leader of the other Democratic party, Kim Young Sam.

The point is that the two Kims did not combine their opposition, so Roh Tae Woo won the 1987 election with 36 percent of the vote. The two opposition candidates had about 26 percent each. As a minority president, however, Roh was unable to control the national legislative body. As a result, with the cooperation of the other conservative parties (about 80 percent of the vote in Korea goes to conservative parties), Roh amalgamated the opposition and changed the name of the ruling party to the Liberal Democratic party and, in effect, negated the split ballot.

Many people were annoyed with Roh Tae Woo obtaining power in this fashion. This is the kind of thing you normally expect, however, in a parliamentary government: If no one has a majority, you get the others to amalgamate to create a 50 percent-plus leader. In any case, that is what happened, and over the last four years, Roh Tae Woo has run a relatively successful government in Korean terms.

People are now beginning to assess what has taken place, and whether democracy has gone forward, stood still, or gone backward. It is a very difficult thing to judge. The process has become more deeply rooted over the past four years, but it is a very new and young experience.

The South Koreans have to figure out once again how to transfer power without riots and revolution. They seem to think that they have the formula, but it has some eerie aspects that remind one of what is happening in the United States. The parties have elected their representatives, and a new party has appeared. It is based more or less on the Ross Perot complaint that business interests aren't being properly served and that the government is not decisive enough and so on.

An interesting thing has happened. Three groups will be involved in the next election. The ruling party is led by Kim Young Sam, who ran before but from a different party. In the opposition is the perennial New Korea Democratic party led by Kim Dae Jung, and a new party called the Reunification Democratic party, under one of the grand old men of the *Chaebol*. Preliminary polls show that Kim Young Sam will get around 45 percent of the vote; Kim Dae Jung, maybe 25 percent; and Chung's party, something like 14 percent. That election will be held at the end of 1992. One of the difficulties with those figures, however, is that the Koreans have learned over the years to be rather closemouthed with pollsters. So one doesn't really know if they are telling you what they believe.

The situation for Korean democracy looks rather favorable, but there are some other points that I want to raise. Fortunately, the situation in Thailand has resolved itself in a good way, but it demonstrates what happened in Korea ten years earlier when the social and political structure of the government had grown out of the army format. Thailand has been ruled by a gang of toughs since

48

1932, and they have tried to keep power exclusively in their hands. Periodically an alleged democrat has been elected, but then the army hasn't liked him and they have thrown him out. The issue is the control of the economy and the wealth of the country. As we have seen, however, archaic forms of authoritarian government cannot go on forever; there comes a time when that kind of thing no longer works.

Nonetheless, we also have to look at trends in the United States, including such events as the May riots in Los Angeles, and consider whether our slogans of democracy will continue to sustain us or whether we may have to make some modifications.

To oversimplify, as we Jefferson admirers realize, ours is an evolutionary situation, and the notion that all men are created equal, except on a very narrow religious and biological basis, seems harder to sustain as we look at our society in general. Does everyone really have an opportunity for equal treatment? We like to talk about everyone being equal at the starting line, but if we actually examined everyone lined up at the race track, we could probably guess who would be the winners and who would be the losers before the race began. A happy notion exists, however, that everything is inevitably getting better on the democratic scene, that equality and freedom is just a blip, and that new models can perhaps overcome some of the old injustices.

There is also a rather dangerous theory afloat that has a lot to do with the immediate problems that exist in Korea. The idea is that there is a certain inevitability in the development and prosperity of democracy once it gets under way. I will give you an easy example.

Francis Fukuyama's book, *The End of History and the Last Man,* uses a familiar argument that Marx also used, namely, that the dialectic of history—the thesis-antithesis and the new synthesis—is forever moving onward and upward. Why he still thinks that is a mystery to me, even though he explained it in great detail in New York a few months ago. Marxism and communism, as we have seen, were left in total disarray through the false belief that one can guide history. Fukuyama uses the arguments of Hegel, an 18th century philosopher, who believed in a progression of universal history.

49

By the time Hegel died, he had located his progression of history somewhere in Jena, in what used to be East Germany. Fukuyama now finds it located in the Western democracies. The idea of the inevitability of democracy, it seems to me, has been totally discredited, hopefully for good. Most of us know that if we don't pay attention to the processes of democracy, there is no reason that it cannot slip backward. There are many examples of that in Latin America, Africa, and perhaps some Asian countries. For this reason, we have to work very hard on democracy.

Others who have written on the moral problems of democracy have asserted that the purpose of the state is to let people fulfill themselves, that there is no point in having a democratic state if it doesn't promote virtuous people and virtuous government. All of us who live in democracies need to keep testing the roots and bases of democracy to be sure that the purpose of democratic government is actually being realized for everyone. The Koreans are going to have to do some rethinking about what has resulted from a democratic form of government and whether it is actually making opportunity available and apparent in the citizenship at large.

The *New York Times Magazine* a few months ago ran an article on Korea in which it concluded that except for the perennial human rights problems in South Korea—which are nothing compared to those in the North and which can be explained, if not totally justified, by the notion that there is still war with the North— President Roh Tae Woo's report card is generally very favorable in Korean terms. It would be no exaggeration to say that if these trends continue after Roh leaves office, the odds are that Korea will continue under a democratic bent, despite its continuing Confucian past, which deals with the world in a hierarchial way. It is an interesting comparison to what is happening in the United States.

Many are familiar with a book entitled *The Radicalism of the American Revolution* by Gordon S. Wood, a Brown University professor of American history, about the radical nature of the American Revolution. The War for Independence with the British was truly dramatic in terms of the institutions that didn't exist previously and those that were totally wiped out. Briefly, his argument is that the colonies, by definition, were a hierarchical group in which people tended to know those above them and those

50

below them, but they didn't know as much on a horizontal or democratic basis about what was going on. Because of commerce in the countryside during the course of the war and early into the 19th century, there were changes in attitude that had been strong in the colonies even before the war—of the notion that I am as good as you, with many exceptions on the top and bottom. By 1835, when Tocqueville came here, a situation had developed such that the first line of his book on *Democracy in America*—and he is speaking from a European aristocratic background—was that he had never before seen such an equality of opportunity. He was amazed by that. It was the most striking thing that he saw in the United States.

To see that it is possible, in a historical sense, to move quickly from a hierarchical view of the world to a democratic, egalitarian one is a hopeful sign that in places like Korea and someday even in Japan or perhaps China, the egalitarian tradition will win out over hierarchical ideas and that the possibilities for all of those countries in terms of democratic development and the liberties that spring from it will finally be realized. I am hopeful that the Koreans will take advantage of traditions that have developed elsewhere. We will see in the election of December 1992 which parties prevail, how they will deal with the potential problem of a president elected by less than half of the people again, whether that will result in another constitutional change regarding the parliamentary system, or whether political tendencies will somehow congeal to enable more steady and rapid progress. I think it is worthwhile to speculate not only about Korean democracy, but also about our own and that of places like Eastern Europe; about how it will all work out and whether the experience of one country might aid the struggle of another; or whether these events are more separate than people such as myself would like to believe.

QUESTION: President Roh Tae Woo's main foreign policy theme is the recognition of the two Koreas by China and the United States. What are the prospects for diplomatic normalization between North Korea and the United States? Would that be a first step toward full recognition?

MR. MYERS: North and South Korea have been engaged for some time in trying to find a formula for unification. That argument has gone on since the end of the Korean War, but the possibilities for reunification have been enormously strengthened by the collapse of the former Soviet Union. North Korea was pretty much dependent on the Soviet Union for oil, all of its military equipment, and a market, so its position has been greatly weakened.

Over the last three or four years, a few official meetings have taken place between North and South Korean officials. They are now meeting more frequently. When I was in Seoul earlier this month, the South Koreans were having their seventh prime minister-level meeting with the North Koreans. It is interesting to compare the funny negotiations taking place between the People's Republic of China and Taiwan. In that case, there are no talks, but rather billions of dollars worth of trade. With the two Koreas, there is plenty of talk, but no exchange of commercial products, even though some of the conglomerate leaders from South Korea have gone north to talk about such trade.

The difficulty with negotiations is that the formula for reunification is not at all clear. The North, despite its crumbling economy and the ideological blow suffered from the collapse of communism in the Soviet Union, is holding off for very tough terms. Moreover, the amount of distrust between the two sides is so great that it takes a real optimist to expect any particular progress.

I am not terribly optimistic about anything happening as long as Roh Tae Woo is in office, because it would be a big boost for him domestically if he could beat North Korean leader Kim Il Sung, in a symbolic way. That would help Roh Tae Woo because roughly 15 percent of the population in South Korea migrated from the North during the Korean war.

All that was agreed to in May—although it does serve as a good precedent—was a visitor exchange involving elderly people from the North and from the South. It was sort of a humanitarian gesture. No specific agreements were reached in terms of commerce, however, and there was no give on the nuclear weapons issue. As you know, North Korea is suspected or accused of building nuclear weapons in a plant north of Pyongyang. At the same time, on a positive note, North Korea has agreed to inspection by the International Atomic Energy Agency, which actually sent some people up there about a month ago. This is a little like the Iraq problem, however. The North Koreans say that they are complying, but they have established a deserved international reputation for digging tunnels into the demilitarized zone and for putting in underground factories and air bases and the like. As a result, the agreement will be inconclusive.

COMMENT: I have been studying in the United States for nine months. I used to think that 200 years of United States history was nothing compared to more than 4,000 years of Korean history. Now that I have studied it some, I have changed my view. In terms of the continuity of the constitutional system, I think the United States has the longest history with the exception of England. In South Korea the democratic system was founded in 1948, so it has less than 50 years of history, and Korea has changed its constitution eight times. So Korea has a short history. Given 4,000 years of a monarchical state and just 50 years of a democratic system, I hope that the United States will approach its relations with Korea with more understanding about Korean culture.

MR. MYERS: That is an important observation. Historically, Korea has been the bridge between China and Japan, and that has not always been a happy situation. According to a Korean proverb, when the whales clash, the shrimp tremble.

If you look at the map, Korea is in between China and Japan, and the United States, its current ally, is a long way away. The Japanese have periodically invaded Korea, and in the 16th century Hideyoshi, the Japanese Shogun, took his armies into Korea and slaughtered its people in a terrible fashion. In Kyoto, Japan, one can still find a mound of ears that he saw fit to send back. The Japanese say little about that anymore. The Chinese Ming Dynasty had to send in troops, and many attribute the decline and overthrow of that dynasty to the wars with Hideyoshi, whom the Koreans and their navy finally turned back on two occasions. But the wars devastated the country. In the late 19th century, the Chinese, Russians, and the Japanese were also conniving over how to take over Korea. The Japanese finally did in 1910 by marching in an army, and in the days before collective security, the incident passed without much attention.

World War II was another tragedy for Korea. The State Department and the now deceased John Allison in particular were afraid that if President Roosevelt and Harry Hopkins brought up the issue of Korea at Yalta with Stalin, and Stalin asked for it, Roosevelt and Hopkins would say fine, because probably neither had ever heard of Korea. Thus, that issue was not discussed, and it remained unsettled until the war was officially over. Then, through telegrams between Stalin and Truman, Korea was arbitrarily divided at the 38th parallel. That division set into play a history with which you are more familiar—the Korean War and its unsatisfactory outcome. Now the Koreans, themselves, are trying to resolve the problem, and while others can help, that is the only way it will ever be successfully resolved.

QUESTION: I understand that we still have troops in Korea. Is that an ongoing situation, and what is behind it?

MR. MYERS: What is behind it is a persistent yet outmoded notion of American security in the Pacific, which explains why we have even more troops in Japan. The problem is that because the war remains unresolved and is still officially on, the North could again attack the South. The American strategy is that with about 40,000 U.S. troops in Korea, the North is unlikely to attack. That security provides a chance for the longer process of negotiation to take place; the Chinese and North Koreans want a settlement.

The Japanese position on this question is very ambiguous. I am not sure that they want a united Korea, and the way they act suggests that they don't. If Korea were united, its population would be roughly 65 million. There are approximately 43 million people in the South and a little over 20 million in the North. Unification would produce a more substantial and powerful group because resources from the North, particularly coal, minerals, and uranium, would be put into the manufacturing and agricultural base of the South. Korea is plagued by many international political complications.

As for the United States, it has been gradually withdrawing troops from Korea. In the longer term—say, ten years—I believe there will be only a very small, if any, American military presence there, because one of the conditions of unification undoubtedly will be the withdrawal of American forces from the South. That will probably serve future U.S. interests well.

QUESTION: In view of the enormously difficult and extremely costly problems of German unification, why would the South Koreans want to take on the burden of bringing in the Northerners?

MR. MYERS: You have put your finger on a very important point. A couple of years ago, there was a lot of enthusiasm in the South for unification, but having seen the problems that the West Germans have run into, the South now has very little enthusiasm. The idea of any substantial proportion of the 20 million North Koreans coming to the South fills them with a certain amount of fear and apprehension in terms of how they could conceivably afford it. That may change over the next 10 or 15 years, because there is a growing labor shortage in the South, and they don't like to import foreign workers on the same principle that the Japanese don't like to import workers. So, South Korea could, perhaps, absorb larger numbers of Korean workers over time.

Still, the disparities are so great. The average South Korean earns something like $6,500 per year, but it is hard to calculate anything in cash in the North because it doesn't run on such a system. Everything is totally subsidized and money is not of much use. That is one difficulty holding back unification. It is also true that for a while the North Koreans feared the East German model, because it would overrun the country and they would lose whatever power and prestige they had. As the South has looked at that model closer, it has also backed off.

QUESTION: Do South Korean students support unification?

MR. MYERS: The students are for Korean unification, and they have tried to arrange exchanges. They have gotten to know the

North Korean situation better and basically welcome the idea of unconditional reunification.

Some years ago the students engaged in riots on this question. They wanted to go through the DMZ, and they gave the government a great deal of trouble, but I don't see that happening anymore.

QUESTION: You have raised some very troubling questions with disarming gentleness. A delegation from Russia was here some time ago, and one of the questions addressed to them concerned what was being done to educate the Russian people to the idea of a democracy or republic. Also, a book published recently under the auspices of the Miller Center raised the issue of whether a republican form of government could be effective and sustainable across a large and populous country, as Mr. Jefferson proposed. Mr. Madison, of course, argued against that and had his way. Finally, a previous speaker here quoted Marvin Kalb as saying that the institution of television was performing a role not envisioned by the Constitution, and in a way that it was not qualified to do. You compared the division in Korea between the North and South to the potential division in this country. Are you anticipating further agitation on the side of division in this country?

MR. MYERS: I wouldn't necessarily make that connection. My point concerned not the North and the South but South Korea itself and the traditional, hierarchical society that has existed there for thousands of years. What type of democracy is possible given such a history? Japan has also faced this question. I mentioned our own revolution as having dramatically changed a hierarchical order into a democratic one, and I wondered whether that example makes it more likely that a place like Korea, which had a hierarchical order for so long, might succeed with a more egalitarian regime. It is problematic, and I'm not sure that they will be able to accomplish such a transformation.

I urge them to look at our example. When you turn to current U.S. society, it seems that despite our intentions and laws, the equality and freedom ideal is not being perfectly met. I don't see how it can be. We will really have to work hard or we may have to consider the notion that we have the wrong model; maybe we are creating problems if a hierarchical world is the reality.

QUESTION: How would you evaluate American policy over the last couple of years towards North Korea, and what role do you see the United States playing during the 1990s in promoting unification?

MR. MYERS: Unification will have to evolve from the two Koreas themselves. Our input is not unimportant, but I don't think it will be decisive.

We are, as I mentioned, South Korea's great but distant friend. The Koreans have found that those are the kinds of friends on whom they like to rely because a history of trying to deal with the Chinese and the Russians suggests that—sort of like Machiavelli's principle—one shouldn't align with a greater power. The Koreans have had a lot of trouble playing all of these people off against each other.

If the two Koreas want unification and can get some guarantees and assurances from their neighbors—and they are a tough group: Japan, China, and Russia—the United States may be able to act as a guarantor for the Koreans and lend some validity to the agreement. However, I don't think that outside powers will be able to play much more of a role than that. The Koreans are very stubborn and difficult people when it comes to negotiating. Their idea of negotiation is that, if you compromise with a political opponent, someone must be buying you off. There is no notion of the opposition being able to team up with the ruling party or vice versa. So I think we are very much beholden to what the two Koreas will do.

I am becoming a little more optimistic about the prospects for unification. I had an opportunity to witness a meeting between the two delegations that included both prime ministers, and there seemed to be a greater semblance of civility than I had anticipated. Both sides know what they want and both will bargain as well as they can. We can't really push them very much. I suppose that we could push the South a little because of the U.S. troops there, but that would probably use up the good will that exists and thus would be counterproductive.

QUESTION: You made an interesting comparison in regard to the contacts between the two opposing regimes. You noted that in contrast to Korea, Taiwan and mainland China have had little official contact, but that economic relations and trade have flourished between the two. Do you think that might be the best model for the two opposing systems to eventually unify: first emphasizing economics, and then politics?

MR. MYERS: There was a little better chance of that working before the collapse of the former Soviet Union, when North Korea's economy was better, having been propped up by free Soviet oil and so on. Now that North Korea's economic position is so desperate, while their military capability is still on a par with the South, they will play the military game to the end. Taiwan, on the other hand, is no military match for the People's Republic of China. They have to go with their strength, and that is trade. When North Korea's military power, through obsolescence, begins to go downhill, then there will be some movement. I don't think unification will be achieved on an economic basis, however.

NARRATOR: We thank Dr. Myers very much for introducing us to some of the realities in Korea. It is important, as one considers problems like Korea, to think about the broader issues of democracy, freedom, and equality. For both the specific discussion and the wider application, we are grateful to you.

II.

THE KOREAN WAR

CHAPTER FOUR

Stalin's Political Objectives in the Korean War: New Documentary Evidence[*]

YOUNGHO KIM

NARRATOR: Youngho Kim has already emerged as one of the bright lights among American and foreign students at the University of Virginia. There are many outstanding foreign students who are intensely interested in the facts, but only a few go on to construct a theory and ask why and how. From almost the first week of his studies at U.Va., it was obvious that Youngho Kim was one of those few.

Mr. Kim is every inch the scholar in attacking both the evidence and the underlying assumptions with which people view the evidence. Looking forward to a professorship in his country or a high position in government, if not both, he is likely to become a major theorist in the field of foreign policy and international relations. From the beginning, Mr. Kim's most compelling interest has been in the origins of the Korean War and Stalin's political objectives. He has conducted archival research at a number of archives and libraries, including the National Archives in Washington, National Records Center, National Archives II, Harry S. Truman Library, and Yale University Library, and has examined new materials—Soviet and Chinese—that have recently become available. Readers will remember his article on the subject in the

---

[*]*Presented in a Forum at the Miller Center of Public Affairs on 7 September 1995.*

Miller Center Journal entitled "Realism: The Paradigmatic Interpretation of International Politics." In fact, Lawrence Eagleburger and General Brent Scowcroft are currently reading his paper as an example of theory and practice. With it, we hope to overthrow the idea that theorists and practitioners can never talk to one another. In medicine, one often hears it said, "Medical research is never too far from the patient in the bed." International relations and government studies could take a page from that approach. Youngho Kim's discussion of Stalin's political objectives in the Korean War can help to close the deep divide separating theorists and practitioners.

MR. KIM: Until recently, the Korean War was "the forgotten war." The dedication of the Korean War Memorial and the recent declassification of important documents, however, have renewed interest in what happened in Korea. For example, one of the most important Soviet sources to become available is a collection of Soviet documents on the war that Russian President Boris Yeltsin handed over to President Kim Young Sam of the Republic of Korea in July 1994. Most of the documents are secret telegrams exchanged between Moscow and Pyongyang, the capital city of North Korea. The collection also includes memoranda of conversations between North Korean leaders and Soviet diplomats, letters from Kim Il Sung to Stalin, and resolutions of the Soviet Politburo.

My presentation draws upon this collection in answering the following three questions. First, who decided to go to war in Korea? Was it Stalin or Kim Il Sung, the North Korean leader? The new documents suggest that Stalin made that decision. Second, why did Stalin decide to approve and support the North Korean invasion against South Korea in late January 1950? I argue that Stalin's decision was guided by the Soviet national interest. The Korean War was part of Stalin's rollback policies, which were designed to check and reduce the power and prestige of the United States in the global Cold War power struggle.

Stalin's definition of the Soviet national interest in terms of prestige leads to my third question: Why does prestige matter in international politics? Drawing on Hans J. Morgenthau, a pioneer in the discipline of international politics, I argue that prestige, meaning a reputation for power, constitutes an essential element of power in international politics. Power has two different aspects: material and psychological. Since prestige represents one of the most important psychological aspects of power, it mattered both to the United States and the Soviet Union in Korea.

Before elaborating upon my answers to these questions, a brief history of Korea leading to the outbreak of the war might be helpful. Japan annexed Korea in 1910. After 36 years, Japanese colonial rule ended when Japan surrendered to the Allied forces. On the hectic night of 10 and 11 August 1945, two U.S. colonels, Dean Rusk and C. H. Bonesteel at the War Department, were asked to find an appropriate dividing line on the Korean Peninsula between U.S.- and Soviet-occupied Korea, north of which the Soviet Union would receive the surrender of remaining Japanese forces in Korea and Manchuria and south of which the United States would do the same. They recommended the now-famous 38th parallel as the dividing line. The United States then occupied the area south of the parallel and the Soviet Union occupied the area north of it. In his memorandum written just after the outbreak of the Korean War, Dean Rusk recalled that he recommended the 38th parallel because Seoul, the capital city of Korea, and Inchon, the main port near Seoul, were included in the area of American responsibility.

After the occupation of Korea, the two superpowers failed to reach an agreement on the establishment of a provisional Korean government that would represent the whole Korean nation despite 62 secret meetings of a U.S.-Soviet Joint Commission. After the failure of the Joint Commission, the United States submitted the Korean problem to the United Nations for resolution. The United Nations then decided to hold elections for all of Korea, but the Soviet occupation command denied entry to the U.N. delegation that was to supervise the elections in the north. As a result, elections under U.N. supervision were held only in South Korea. The Republic of Korea was established in the south in August 1948, and the Democratic People's Republic of Korea emerged in the north. Thus, the division of Korea was consolidated with the emergence of two ideologically hostile, separate regimes. Soviet occupation forces withdrew from the North in December 1948, and

U.S. occupation forces left Korea by 30 June 1949. The United States left behind a military advisory group of roughly 500 and officially gave diplomatic recognition to South Korea. Similarly, Soviet military advisers remained in North Korea with the opening of the Soviet Embassy in Pyongyang. The Soviet advisory group, including the members of the embassy, numbered more than 3,000.

KIM IL SUNG'S ONGJIN OCCUPATION PLAN

Having given this brief summary of the history leading up to the war, I will now address the first question: Was the decision to launch the war made in Moscow or Pyongyang? Who had made the decision? To answer this question, I will begin by analyzing Kim Il Sung's Ongjin occupation plan.

The region from the Ongjin Peninsula to the city of Kaesong constitutes the westernmost sector of the 38th parallel when the parallel was divided into four sectors. The central sector extends from Kaesong to Chunchon. The mountainous areas are located between Chunchon and the east coast. The easternmost sector extends from the mountainous areas to the east coast. Since there were no inland roads to the peninsula from the South, Ongjin was cut off from the rest of South Korea. South Korean military troops and supplies had to be brought by sea from the port of Inchon. From Inchon, 12 hours were required to reinforce Southern troops and bring supplies by sea, whereas the Northern resupply base was just one hour away by road. Thus, the South was at a strategic disadvantage on the Ongjin Peninsula. This strategic advantage for the North was not overlooked by Kim Il Sung. Recently declassified Soviet documents confirm that Kim Il Sung advocated the occupation of the Ongjin Peninsula just after the withdrawal of U.S. forces from South Korea in late June 1949.

Through an analysis of Kim's occupation plan, one can develop the following scenario: The North provokes the South in an attempt to occupy the Ongjin Peninsula, the South counterattacks, and the war spreads from Ongjin eastward to Chorwon, Kumhwa, and Yangyang on the east coast. This scenario was highly probable

64

because South Korean leaders considered the defense of the Ongjin Peninsula vital to the security of South Korea.

President Syngman Rhee of South Korea, for example, expressed his determination to defend the Ongjin Peninsula. He said that South Korea would reinforce a large number of forces to defend Ongjin "whenever the misguided people of the North . . . encroach on that part of Korea which is governed by Koreans." With respect to defending Ongjin in case of a North Korean attempt to capture the region, "the [South Korean] military [leaders] were insistent that the only way to relieve pressure on Ongjin would be to drive North. The South Korean military urged mounting an immediate attack north towards Charwon [sic-Chorwon]." Because the city of Chorwon was located 20 miles north of the 38th parallel, Kim's Ongjin attack plan had the possibility of bringing about a general war between the North and South. If Kim had planned and executed the Ongjin occupation and created the political and military situations in which general war between the North and South would occur, then one might be able to conclude that Kim made the decision to go to war in Korea. According to this scenario, the Soviet Union and the United States would team up with their respective Korean allies only after the war on the Korean Peninsula had already erupted. The Soviet Union and the United States would have had no prior knowledge that general war would break out.

In contrast to this scenario in which Kim Il Sung plans and executes the Ongjin occupation, an alternative scenario suggests that Stalin would not permit Kim Il Sung to occupy the Ongjin Peninsula if Kim's plan were not in accordance with the Soviet global Cold War strategy. In other words, the Ongjin attack or a general war would begin only when and where Stalin regarded it as contributing to the Soviet national interest. Stalin would hold Kim back until the emergence of what Stalin himself considered a more auspicious strategic environment in the Far East. If this alternative scenario is the true one, one can conclude that Stalin dominated the decision-making process to pursue his own political objectives. An analysis of these two competing scenarios is therefore necessary to identify the locus of the decision to go to war in Korea.

Ten days before Kim presented the Ongjin occupation plan to Terrenty F. Shtykov, the Soviet ambassador to North Korea, the North launched a major attack on three points on the Ongjin Peninsula—Turak Mountain, Undong, and Kuksa Height—at 5:00 a.m. on 4 August 1949. The attack was probably launched to demonstrate the military feasibility of North Korean troops occupying the region. The North mobilized less than one or two battalions in most of the border clashes in the past, yet the 4 August attack involved approximately two regiments supported by artillery units.

On 14 August 1949, Kim proposed the Ongjin occupation plan in a meeting with Ambassador Shtykov. Kim's plan was succinctly summarized in the report of Grigorii I. Tunkin, counselor of the Soviet Embassy in Pyongyang:

The [Ongjin attack] proposal of Kim Il Sung amounts to the following: at the beginning to strike the South Korean army on the Ongjin Peninsula, to destroy the two regiments located there, to occupy the territory of the peninsula and the territory to the east of it, for example to Kaidzio [Kaesong], and then to see what to do further. After this blow the South Korean army may become demoralized. In this case move further to the south. If the South Korean army is not demoralized as a result of the Ongjin operation, to seal the borders seized, to shorten in that way, the line of defense approximately by one third [that is, 120 km].

Because Shtykov did not have the authority to decide Soviet policies without prior consultation with Stalin—Shtykov was a post office for Stalin in North Korea (laughter)—he promised to relay Kim's plan to Stalin.

STALIN'S RESPONSE TO KIM'S ONGJIN OCCUPATION PLAN

On 27 August 1949, Shtykov reported to Stalin Kim's plans to occupy the Ongjin Peninsula and, if the situations permitted, to

66

invade the South. In the briefing, Shtykov advanced the view that the North should not be permitted to invade the South, citing the existence of two internationally recognized states on the peninsula. The possibility that the United States would intervene to support the South could not be excluded. Furthermore, Shtykov cited the failure of the North to secure predominant military capabilities over the South. Shtykov argued that the Ongjin plan was militarily feasible, but the operations could turn into a prolonged war if the South counterattacked.

In the absence of Ambassador Shtykov, Kim Il Sung, anxious to know the views of Stalin on the Ongjin plan, ordered his personal secretary and Russian translator, Mun Il, to see Counselor Tunkin on 3 September 1949. Mun repeated Kim's Ongjin occupation plan, adding that "Kim Il Sung is convinced that they [North Koreans] are in a position to seize South Korea in the course of two weeks, maximum two months," given favorable international circumstances after the Ongjin operations. "Favorable international circumstances" probably meant American nonintervention.

Upon the receipt of Tunkin's report of 3 September, Andrei Gromyko, deputy minister of foreign affairs of the Soviet Union, instructed Tunkin to meet Kim and answer questions related to Kim's Ongjin occupation plan. The next day Tunkin met Kim and reported the results of the meeting and his own recommendations to Moscow. Tunkin reported that Kim's Ongjin plan would result in a civil war between the North and South because most of the leaders of the two Koreas supported reunification through force. Tunkin's analysis anticipated the development of a general war as a result of Kim's occupation attempt. Counselor Tunkin recommended that the Soviet Union should not permit Kim to execute the Ongjin occupation plan.

In addition to the possibility of a general war between the North and South, Tunkin also objected to Kim's request to occupy Ongjin because of the impossibility of a speedy victory of the North. He believed that the Ongjin attack would lead to a prolonged war if the North failed to secure a military predominance over the South. Moreover, he did not exclude the possibility of direct American intervention to rescue the South when the Ongjin operations developed into a prolonged war. Thus, Tunkin concluded that the North must not be permitted to launch the Ongjin attack, not to mention invade the South.

After Stalin reviewed the recommendations of Ambassador Shtykov and Counselor Tunkin, the final decision on Kim's invasion and Ongjin occupation plans was made and sent to Kim Il Sung. The Politburo decision stated that the North was not militarily prepared for an invasion and that the lack of North Korean military superiority over the South would lead to a prolonged war.

On the Ongjin occupation plan, the Politburo decision stated:

> As regards a partial operation to seize Ongjin Peninsula and the region of Kaesong, as a result of which the borders of North Korea would be moved almost to Seoul itself, it is impossible to view this operation other than as the beginning of a war between North and South Korea, for which North Korea is not prepared either militarily or politically.

As I have illustrated, South Korean political and military leaders would not have permitted the North to occupy the Ongjin Peninsula. The South Korean Army would have driven north to take Chorwon or other cities north of the parallel in an attempt to take pressure off the Ongjin Peninsula. The analysis of the Soviet Politburo on the Korean situation reflected concerns about the Ongjin attack developing into a general war between the North and South. The Politburo decision therefore rejected Kim's occupation plan because the North was not prepared for a general war with the South.

Another important example shows how Stalin put tight reins on Kim until the emergence of a more auspicious strategic environment for the Soviet Union in the Far East. Stalin's dominant role in the Korea decision can be seen in his handling of a major border incident that took place contrary to the order of the Politburo decision of September 1949.

The North launched a massive attack on the strategic Unpa Mountain on the Ongjin Peninsula on 14 October 1949. Soviet advisers were directly involved in the operations. After this border incident, a proposal was made to the Politburo to investigate whether Ambassador Shtykov had faithfully carried out its decision of 24 September 1949, which prohibited Kim from provoking a major border incident. Gromyko repeated this warning to Shtykov in a telegram dated 27 October 1949:

It was forbidden to you to recommend to the government of North Korea that they carry out active operations against the South Koreans without approval of the Center [that is, Stalin], and it was indicated to you that it was necessary that you present to the Center timely reports on all actions which are being planned and events which are occurring along the 38th parallel.

After the order was delivered to Shtykov and Kim Il Sung, no major border fighting along the 38th parallel occurred until the outbreak of the war in June 1950.

This drop in major border incidents was noted in intelligence reports of the Far East Command under General MacArthur. I have checked U.S. intelligence reports from October 1949 to February 1950 in the archives. The intelligence reports recorded that "all incidents were of a minor nature" during this period. I cite intelligence reports up to 14 February 1950 because Stalin expressed his desire to approve the North Korean invasion on 30 January 1950. After that date, no major border incidents occurred. Stalin's response to the October Ongjin incident and the decreased provocation by the North demonstrate that Stalin sought to curtail border incidents that might flare up into a general war between the North and South until a more auspicious moment could be found.

In summary, an analysis of Kim's Ongjin occupation plan and Stalin's response demonstrates that Stalin gauged the North Korean invasion in light of Soviet national interests and that the transfer of the decision from Stalin to Kim never happened. Only when the timing was right did Stalin capitalize on the irredentist zeal of Kim Il Sung to reunify the Korean nation by the use of force and approve the North Korean invasion to pursue Soviet national interests.

69

THE MOMENT OF DECISION FOR STALIN

For Stalin, the moment of decision came in December 1949, when Mao visited Moscow to negotiate the Sino-Soviet Treaty of Friendship, Alliance, and Mutual Assistance. Before the visit, two events occurred that influenced Stalin's calculations with respect to Korea. First, the Soviet Union exploded its first atomic bomb in August 1949, ending America's nuclear monopoly. Despite the low stockpiles, Soviet nuclear capability may have emboldened Stalin. The second incident to influence Stalin's assessment of the Korean situation was the Chinese Communist victory in the Chinese civil war, which led to the establishment of the People's Republic of China (PRC) in October 1949. The establishment of the PRC contributed to the emergence of what one historian has called a "transnational network" embracing North Korea, Manchuria, and the Soviet Far East. Stalin sought to consolidate the North Korean-Manchurian-Soviet Far Eastern region into a "strategic complex." The consolidation of this strategic complex was made possible through a secret protocol to the main Sino-Soviet Treaty. The existence of a secret protocol was widely rumored but not confirmed until 1989.

The secret protocol stipulated that the citizens of third countries such as the United States and Britain were not allowed to "settle or carry out any industrial, financial, trade, or other related activities in Manchuria and Xinjiang, and [that] the Soviet Union would impose comparable restrictions on the Soviet Far East and the Central Asian republics." The agreement cleared Manchuria of any outside interference. Stalin's attempt to consolidate the strategic complex before the Korean War demonstrates his careful attention to creating an advantageous strategic environment in the Far East.

This strategic complex would appear as a formidable threat when MacArthur demanded the expansion of hostilities into Manchuria after the defeat of the U.N. offensive of 24 November 1950. One observer noted that expansion of the war in Stalin's strategic complex meant "slowly sinking in the quagmire of that vast waste over which no victory could be anything but Pyrrhic." In

70

short, Stalin's decision to approve Kim's plan was not "reckless war-making of the worst kind" as some scholars claim, but rather a carefully laid trap.

THE SECOND QUESTION:
DEFINITION OF SOVIET NATIONAL INTEREST

Now to the second question: How did Stalin define Soviet national interest in the decision to approve and support the North Korean invasion? In my view, Stalin's most important objective was to deal a *severe* blow to the prestige of the United States. Gaining South Korea "by American default," in Truman's terms, was not sufficient to achieve Stalin's purpose. Maximum prestige would only be gained if the United States were defeated and forced out of Korea after its military intervention in the war.

Stalin's telegram to Mao Zedong provides an important clue toward explaining Stalin's definition of the Soviet national interest in terms of prestige. This telegram was written sometime after 29 September 1950. In this telegram Stalin suggests his political motive in his analysis of the reasons for American intervention:

The U.S.A. might be drawn into a major war out of [concern for its] prestige; China will consequently be drawn into war and at the same time the U.S.S.R. will be drawn into war, since it is tied to China by a mutual assistance pact.

Stalin's analysis of the reasons for American intervention in the war was a mirror image of Soviet national interest. Stalin was concerned about the prestige of the Soviet Union in the global Cold War power struggle with the United States because prestige as "the reputation for power" constitutes an important component of power in international politics.

In addition, Stalin sanctioned the war on the Korean Peninsula because he believed that the war would diminish the role of the United States in the global struggle for power. The removal of South Korea from the U.S. sphere of influence would have dealt a blow to the prestige of the United States, which had played the dominant role in the creation of South Korea. For this reason, I consider the Korean War a part of Stalin's rollback policies.

Stalin's rollback was limited geographically to the Korean Peninsula. This limitation does not mean that Stalin was simply interested in the incorporation of South Korean territories into the Soviet orbit. Stalin expected to undermine U.S. prestige by crossing the containment line and, for the first time since the inception of the Cold War, reducing the territories under direct U.S. influence. The erosion of American prestige was perhaps the most important political effect that Stalin sought to achieve.

Thus, for U.S. Secretary of State Dean Acheson, who defined prestige as the shadow cast by power, American intervention was necessary to defeat Stalin's designs because "to back away from this challenge, in view of our [American] capacity of meeting it, would be highly destructive of the power and prestige of the United States."

As Stalin sought to undermine U.S. prestige by rolling South Korea back from under the U.S. sphere of influence, Acheson attempted to defeat the Soviet political objective. Yet for Acheson, the pursuit of U.S. prestige interest had to be achieved without provoking Stalin into a general war. In Acheson's terms, the defeat of the Soviet objective must be achieved "without dropping matches in the powder keg, which would blow the world to smithereens." Thus, the localization of the war was no less important than the defeat of Soviet political objective through direct American intervention.

An analysis of Stalin's and Acheson's views shows that Stalin's concern about Soviet prestige represented the mirror image of Acheson's understanding of U.S. national interests in terms of prestige. In short, the leaders of the two superpowers involved in Korea based their decisions on the same definition of the national interests. Both perceived their national interests in terms of prestige. At the same time, the leaders of both superpowers sought to pursue prestige interest without a general war between them.

Youngho Kim

THE THIRD QUESTION: WHY DOES
PRESTIGE MATTER IN INTERNATIONAL POLITICS?

Moving on to the third question: Why does prestige—a word that comes from the Latin meaning, "juggler's tricks" and "to dazzle the eyes"—matter in international politics? An example from the Korean War should help illustrate what prestige means in international politics. General MacArthur's brilliant and successful Inchon landing on 15 September 1950 during the Korean War resulted in the development of what General Ridgway called "an almost superstitious regard for General MacArthur's infallibility." Why? Recall that the term *prestige* originally meant "to dazzle the eyes." In the same fashion, MacArthur's *dazzling* performance at Inchon heightened his personal prestige. MacArthur's reputation was so elevated that he appeared infallible. Acheson noted that even President Truman made a "pilgrimage" to Wake Island to show his respect for the general. Similarly, Stalin expected that a dazzling victory on Korea would make the Soviet Union look invincible in the Far East and the world.

In his classic book *Politics Among Nations*, Hans J. Morgenthau defines prestige as the "reputation for power." Morgenthau urges the reader to make a clear distinction between the material and psychological aspects of power in international politics. For Morgenthau, the employment of force means the abdication of the psychological aspect of power in favor of the material aspect of power. Moreover, in the exercise of force, there emerges a tendency to lose sight of the importance of the psychological aspect of power, even though the attempt to establish relations of psychological control among nations is a perennial element of power despite its immaterial and intangible nature.

In Morgenthau's view, one of the most important psychological aspects of power is prestige; that is, the reputation for power. In his view, the image of a nation's power in the mirror of other nations constitutes an important component of power. The pursuit of prestige results from the attempt "to impress other nations with the power one's own nation actually possesses, or with the power it believes, or wants the other nations to believe, it possesses."

73

Drawing on Morgenthau's definition of prestige, we can conclude that Stalin's rollback on the Korean Peninsula was designed to deal a severe blow to the prestige of the United States by removing South Korea from the U.S. containment line. The erosion of American prestige means the weakening of the power of the United States because prestige as the reputation for power constitutes an essential element of power in international relations.

CONCLUSIONS

In conclusion, the origins of the Korean War are to be found in Stalin's rollback policies. Stalin defined Soviet national interest in terms of prestige in the Cold War and aimed to achieve his political objective by removing South Korea from the U.S. sphere of influence. He concluded that American prestige would suffer if the United States intervened in Korea and was then forced out. The moment of decision for Stalin came with the Communist victory in China. The emergence of the strategic complex embracing North Korea, Manchuria, and the Soviet Far East led to Stalin's decision to approve the North Korean invasion.

Stalin's rollback policy in Korea had another important aspect. It was a rollback geographically limited to the Korean Peninsula. The limited nature of the war was dictated by the political objective Stalin sought to achieve in Korea. The objective was to undermine the power of the United States without provoking a general war. To this end, Stalin took deliberate measures to conceal direct Soviet involvement in the planning and execution of the war.

Stalin, who had killed millions of innocent Soviet citizens, was unlikely to care much about the calamities visited on the Korean nation if war served his broader political objectives. Stalin therefore capitalized on Kim Il Sung's irredentist zeal to reunify the nation by force to support his own political objective of rolling back the power and prestige of the United States. The United States, however, would respond to Stalin's provocation with its huge war-making capabilities to save South Korea. The intensity of the war and the enormous suffering of Koreans, both North and South, resulted because the Korean Peninsula was turned into a battleground for the two superpowers. Here lies the big difference between Stalin's interest in prestige and U.S. intervention to defeat Stalin's objective in normative terms: Stalin knew how intense the war would be with U.S. intervention and the subsequent mobilization of Communist Chinese forces when he maneuvered to coordinate three Communist countries for the war in Korea.

Stalin's cynical attitude and Kim Il Sung's naiveté combined to bring a disaster unprecedented in the history of the Korean nation. But despite this unprecedented destruction of Korean society, South Korea is now marching toward the turn of the century as a democratic country with a prospering economy. The 54,000 young Americans, to whom the Korean War Memorial is dedicated, did not die in vain. The Korean War should no longer be "the forgotten war."

QUESTION: You present considerable evidence that Stalin vetoed Kim's 1949 desire to strike an attack at the Ongjin Peninsula and invade the South; however, I am not entirely convinced with your argument that Stalin planned the war and why he planned to launch it in June 1950. From your research, what factors were considered, and to what extent did Stalin actually manage the preparation for the war? Also, what evidence exists to support the argument that Stalin chose the Korean War as a way to check what he saw to be the growing power of Communist China?

MR. KIM: To answer your second question, the book *Uncertain Partners: Stalin, Mao, and the Korean War* (1993), written by S. N. Goncharov, John W. Lewis, and Xue Litai, emphasizes the conflict between China and the Soviet Union. After the victory of Mao Zedong in China, these scholars argue that Stalin was concerned about the future of communism in Asia. The recently declassified Soviet and Chinese documents that I read, however, showed no such conflict of interest between Mao Zedong and Stalin. Stalin dominated the decision-making process. At the same time, Stalin approved Kim Il Sung's plan on the condition that Kim discuss the matter with Mao Zedong first. If Mao agreed, then they could go to war in Korea. Hence, it appears that Stalin sought Mao's concurrence and consultation on the issue. Mao, however, was

75

suspicious after meeting Kim Il Sung but ultimately agreed to the North Korean invasion after receiving a personal message from Stalin–the same message Stalin had sent to Kim. Before this Kim-Mao meeting of May 1950, Stalin had already sent General Bashilev, a German-Soviet war hero, to North Korea to draw invasion plans in February 1950.

Though many scholars have portrayed the Korean War as an event that foreshadowed the eventual split between the Soviet Union and China, my research shows Mao and Stalin to be very cooperative during the period that led up to the Korean War. As for your first question, the information from the Soviet side admittedly is very limited. I focused on Stalin's interest in prestige based upon the documents available to me at this time.

QUESTION: Why did the Soviets absent themselves from the United Nations where they could have blocked the United Nations effort in the war?

MR. KIM: According to declassified China documents on the Sino-Soviet Friendship Treaty negotiations between Stalin and Mao, Stalin proposed that Nationalist China be expelled from the United Nations. Knowing that the United States would not approve of the admission of Communist China to the United Nations at that time, Stalin proposed a boycott of the United Nations, and on 8 January 1950, the Soviet Union began to withdraw its representatives from the United Nations. On 13 January 1950, Soviet representatives were withdrawn from the U.N. Security Council as well. All of this maneuvering took place during Sino-Soviet Friendship Treaty negotiations. Whatever Stalin's reasons, it is evident that the boycott of the United Nations was a deliberate move by Stalin.

NARRATOR: Professor Meador, having organized a major conference on the Korean War and given your longtime interest on the subject, what are your comments?

PROFESSOR MEADOR: Do you think that, perhaps, your interpretation of events might be too extreme? Though it is true that Kim Il Sung would not have started the war without Stalin's approval, I question your suggestion that Stalin himself, without any urging from Kim, would have started the Korean War. After all, the war was not Stalin's idea; it was Kim's.

MR. KIM: I do not disregard the importance of the chemistry between Stalin and Kim Il Sung in bringing about a disaster in Korea. The more important issue here is to explain why this particular war broke out at this particular moment. In doing so, we can clarify the political objectives of the initiative. In defense of my interpretation, allow me to draw from Henry Kissinger. Larger powers tend to dominate the decision-making process. For example, Great Britain made a number of proposals during the Korean War, but the United States, because it was the larger power, could reject those proposals it did not like and accept those it found to be in its national interest. Similarly, Stalin was the leader of a country stronger than Kim Il Sung's; thus, Stalin had a greater voice in deciding whether to invade South Korea.

QUESTION: After the fall of the Nationalist government on mainland China. Secretary of State Dean Acheson gave a speech before the National Press Club in which he identified Japan and the Philippines as being vital to the U.S. interest but did not specifically include South Korea. Do you think that Secretary Acheson's failure to include South Korea within the sphere of U.S. defense commitments would have been a significant factor toward making Stalin think he could get away with it, thus emboldening him?

MR. KIM: Secretary Acheson's speech was likely a significant factor in Stalin's decision, but specific documents to prove that fact are lacking. With respect to Acheson's defense perimeter line in the Far East, Acheson's conceptualization was perfectly in accordance with the emergency war plans of the Joint Chiefs of Staff (JCS). Actually, the idea of a defense perimeter was developed by the JCS, not Dean Acheson. President Truman had put strict budget restraints on the defense budget at the time. Thus, the JCS sought to pursue what Walter Lippmann called "solvency" in its planning to balance commitments and resources. This emergency plan was based upon the assumption that the Korean

77

Peninsula would be overrun by the Soviet Union within 20 days after the outbreak of a general war. Any remaining U.S. forces on the Korean Peninsula would then have to withdraw to Japan. The problem with this emergency plan was that it assumed the outbreak of a general war, not a limited war, like Korea. The U.S. government, however, was fortunate that George Kennan, the architect of containment policy, emphasized the imperative for the preparation for a limited war as early as January 1947 and thus prepared the U.S. government for the possibility of a limited war. Though Kennan's plan was not accepted at the time, it was accepted after the outbreak of the Korean War.

QUESTION: Does the state of war still exist in Korea? What mechanism exists to end it?

MR. KIM: One of the most important factors is the stationing of U.S. troops on the Korean Peninsula. Please remember that the Korean War has not officially ended. North Korea, China, and the United Nations signed an armistice treaty in 1953, but there is no peace treaty.

QUESTION: What was Mao's interest in entering the Korean War? Was he also seeking prestige?

MR. KIM: Yes, Mao also sought prestige. In memoranda written at the time, it is clear that President Truman thought the prestige of Communist China after the defeat of U.N. forces in November 1950 to be much too overrated. He thought that Mao's prestige had to be deflated.

NARRATOR: We thank Youngho Kim for his thought-provoking presentation on the origins of the Korean War and Stalin's political objectives.

The author gratefully acknowledges generous grants from the Miller Center of Public Affairs at the University of Virginia, the Harry S. Truman Library Institute, and the Korean-American Scholarship Foundation for the preparation of this presentation.

III.

U.S.-KOREAN AND U.S.-CHINESE RELATIONS

CHAPTER FIVE

U.S.-Korean Relations: Continuity and Change in the Post–Cold War Era*

AMBASSADOR SEUNG-SOO HAN

NARRATOR: Dr. Seung-Soo Han is South Korea's ambassador extraordinary and plenipotentiary to the United States. Before becoming ambassador, Dr. Han had a distinguished career as South Korea's minister of trade and industry (1988-90) and as a member of the ruling party in the National Assembly. As minister of trade and industry, he established new trading relations with the United States and initiated the first International Exposition held in a developing country. He helped rationalize shipbuilding in Korea and headed the Korean parliamentary group that took part in the Uruguay Round. He was also instrumental to the creation of the Asian Pacific Economic Cooperation (APEC) and founded the Korean Academy of Industrial Technology.

Before entering politics, Ambassador Han was professor of economics at Seoul National University from 1970 to 1988. Over the course of his academic career, he has also been a visiting professor at the University of Tokyo, Fulbright Scholar at Harvard, and research officer in the Department of Applied Economics at Cambridge University. At York University, he received his doctorate and served as fellow and lecturer. He is the author of many books, including *The Health of Nations* (1985), *Britain and the*

---

*Presented in a Forum at the Miller Center of Public Affairs on 25 October 1994.

Common Market (1971), *Taxes in Britain and the EEC: the Problem of Harmonisation* (1968), and *The Growth and Function of the European Budget* (1971). His Korean research publications include *Tax Burden Distribution in Korea* and *Deficit Financing in Korea*, and he has recently written a Korean undergraduate textbook, *The Theory of Economic Policy* (1994).

Ambassador Han is highly decorated in Korea and abroad. It is a great pleasure to have him here to continue our ongoing series on Korea.

AMBASSADOR HAN: My topic today is a broad one, and I cannot do it justice in this relatively brief presentation. Moreover, on these occasions, I am always acutely aware of the remark that Winston Churchill supposedly made about Ramsay MacDonald, which is that the leader of the Labor party possessed "the gift of compressing the smallest possible amount of thought into the largest possible number of words." I trust you will not think me similarly gifted today. My aim, instead, is to provide for you a kind of tour d'horizon of U.S.-Korean relations.

For a relationship as close as that of the United States and Korea, its history is a fairly short one. I am not aware that any Americans even visited Korea before the 19th century. Indeed, the first stirrings of American interest in Korea were mainly after-effects of Commodore Matthew Perry's famous voyage to Japan in the 1850s. By the 1870s, however, American businessmen were increasingly interested in Korea for its commercial potential, while American clergymen were interested in Korea for its missionary potential.

Around this time, a newly rising Japan began to press the Korean Kingdom for various concessions. Anxiety grew among the Korean ruling elite about Japan's intentions—whether Japan intended to bring Korea into its sphere of influence, or worse. In retrospect, we know that these fears were all too well founded. The Korean government sought to counterbalance the influence of its Eastern neighbor by negotiating treaties with major powers outside the region, powers that Korea thought were unlikely to endanger its sovereignty. Korea signed the first two such treaties with the United States and Great Britain. The Treaty of Chemulpo, signed in 1882 by the United States and Korea, marked the formal start of the Korea-U.S. relationship. King Kojong's special envoy, Min Young Ik, was sent to America the following year and presented his credentials to President Arthur on 17 September 1883, and our first minister plenipotentiary presented his credentials to President Cleveland on 17 January 1888. At that time, only four countries in Asia had diplomatic relationships with the United States: Korea, China, Japan, and Thailand.

Shortly before the treaty was negotiated, a young Bostonian by the name of Percival Lowell visited Korea and stayed during the winter of 1880–81. Lowell would later become one of the greatest astronomers of his day and the founder of the Lowell Observatory in Arizona. Long before his prestigious career in astronomy, however, he had been an avid student of Oriental culture. After leaving Korea, Lowell wrote a book about his experience and titled it *Chosun: Land of the Morning Calm. Chosun* was the official name of Korea from the 14th century to the early 20th century.

Chosun may well be the first book about Korea written by an American. It is filled with fascinating observations of an era long gone. I was particularly intrigued by his assessment of the commercial aptitude of Koreans. He wrote, "The Koreans are not a shop-keeping people. Shops are few in number and deficient in kind. . . . Trade is not one of the mainsprings to action in men and women in Korea." In fact, for the next seven decades very little commerce took place between the United States and Korea, despite the fact that the official Korea-U.S. protocol of 1882 was titled the "Treaty of Amity and Commerce." At the time, Lowell's assessment of the Korean people might have seemed all too true, but it is nevertheless ironic from today's standpoint.

With the Japanese occupation in 1910 eliminating Korea's diplomatic sovereignty, formal relations between the United States and Korea were suspended, though some American doctors and educators remained in Korea. It was during this time that the future president of the Republic of Korea, Syngman Rhee, organized an independence movement among Korean communities in the United States.

Diplomatic relations immediately resumed following the establishment of the Republic of Korea in 1948. With the outbreak of the Korean War in 1950, our two countries quickly formed a military alliance. After hostilities ended in 1953, American foreign aid flowed into Korea to assist with the postwar reconstruction. The Republic of Korea's per capita income then was on par with that of Somalia, Ethiopia, and Haiti. Korea remained poor and underdeveloped and its foreign trade minimal until the 1960s. Writing in 1965, American journalist John C. Caldwell described Korea as "a land of misery and chaos, a nation unable to help itself because it has no voice in any major decision affecting its future." Compared to Communist North Korea, the Republic of Korea had a much weaker industrial base and lower living standards, and in the 1950s most experts considered the Republic of Korea one of the least promising candidates for successful development.

In the 1960s the Republic of Korea changed course economically. Under the new regime of President Park Chung Hee, Korea's development strategy switched from import-substitution to export-led industrialization. American investment flowed into Korea, and the United States became the major market for the nation's new export industries.

Still, it was only in the 1980s that the Korean economy started to become truly "internationalized" by opening its markets and fully participating in multilateral economic forums. By the end of the decade, Korea even came to be seen as a source of capital by other countries, including former Eastern bloc nations.

During this period, the Korean-U.S. economic partnership also underwent a striking transformation. Before 1980 Korea supplied predominantly labor-intensive products in exchange for capital and agricultural products. Since then, Korea's exports have become considerably more diverse and sophisticated. Korea has opened its markets and widened the range of its exports to include many consumer foods and services. Also in the 1980s, U.S. and Korean firms built up a complicated structure of licensing, contracting, and co-producing that continues to increase in both size and complexity.

A growing trade imbalance became a serious concern for both countries. Many specific areas of disagreement existed, but of particular concern was Korea's burgeoning trade surplus with the United States. Largely due to macroeconomic factors including the overvalued dollar and low oil prices, the bilateral trade surplus peaked at $10 billion in 1987.

When I became minister of trade and industry in late 1988, the level of trade frictions between the two countries was approaching a crisis point. During the first six months of my tenure, defusing these tensions was my top priority. In late spring of 1989 the immediate danger was that the United States would declare Korea to be a "priority foreign country" (PFC), to use the jargon of the famous "Super 301" of the Omnibus Trade Act of 1988. Such action would have branded Korea as an "unfair trader" and would have played directly into the hands of anti-American elements in Korea—a small but vociferous minority. I believe that such a development would have had a dangerous destabilizing impact on the entire bilateral relationship, including the security dimension.

Fortunately, we were able to avoid such an outcome. Almost at the eleventh hour, my negotiating team and its U.S. counterpart worked out a compromise agreement. Our chief negotiator at that time was Assistant Minister Kim Chulsu, who is currently minister of trade and industry, as well as Korea's candidate for the post of director general of the World Trade Organization. In the 1990s, the bilateral trade account returned to relative equilibrium, and not surprisingly, the level of trade frictions has greatly subsided.

We now find ourselves in the post-Cold War era. Some people would date the beginning of this era at November 1989 with the fall of the Berlin Wall; others would say it began with the failure of the hard-line putsch in Moscow in August 1991 or the collapse of the Soviet Union at the end of the year. In fact, the end of the Cold War was probably prefigured by the policies that Gorbachev introduced after his first year or two in office.

That this historic change in the direction of world affairs would necessarily have significant implications for the Korea-U.S. partnership was never in doubt, but the exact nature of those implications is still far from clear. Certainly, our bilateral relationship was profoundly shaped by the early Cold War period. Until the 1960s, that relationship, at least seen from the American side, was above all a military and security alliance. To the degree that the United States had an economic interest in Korea at all, it was to build up South Korea as a "model of free enterprise" in contrast to the Communist North. When Korea began its export-led economic takeoff in the mid-1960s, the United States was delighted that its ally could so quickly transform itself in economic terms from a basket case to a showcase. Korea's success also served to vindicate the "trade, not aid" school of development. With a per capita income of over $7,000, Korea is now the 12th largest trading nation and the 15th largest economy in the world.

The emergence of serious trade frictions in the late 1980s shows that the Cold War ethos was already fading into history. Ten or 15 years earlier, the "Super 301" confrontation of 1989 would never have been allowed to become politicized to the extent that it was. Both sides would have shown more willingness to compromise for the sake of broader strategic interests. By the late 1980s, however, the sense of Cold War tension, of global struggle between ideologically hostile camps, was largely absent; hence, Washington and Seoul felt it was no longer so risky for them to publicly air their grievances with each other.

Also at that time a feeling was prevalent among U.S. policymakers that North Korea was becoming an increasingly irrelevant anachronism—residually dangerous, to be sure, but nevertheless unlikely to stage a major offensive in the absence of support from Moscow and Beijing. Almost no one back then would have predicted the North Korean nuclear crisis of the spring of 1994. After all, Pyongyang had signed the nuclear Non-Proliferation Treaty (NPT), and the Soviet Union was seen to provide a kind of surety for North Korean compliance.

By the beginning of the 1990s, both partners came to accept that trade and economic relations would henceforth develop more or less independently of strategic and security concerns. This development reflected a general international trend in which economic competition was quickly replacing ideological rivalry as the motivating force in world affairs.

Since the 1960s, trade with Korea has become increasingly important to the U.S. economy and American consumers. In recent years, Korea has been America's eighth largest trading partner and the fifth largest importer of U.S. agricultural products (1992: $2.2 billion; 1993: $1.9 billion). Nevertheless, relative to the size of its economy, Korea is obviously much more dependent on the

American market than the United States is on the Korean market. In fact, since the founding of the Republic of Korea in 1948, there has not been a year in which the United States was not Korea's largest trading partner.

Up to a point, dependence on the U.S. market is not bad for Korea. On the contrary, access to the open American market was an essential element in our economic takeoff 30 years ago and remains a precondition of our continued economic success. Rather, the question is one of degree. In the 1980s when the United States took in at least 40 percent of Korea's exports, bilateral trade relations had so high a profile in Korea that they could not help but become entangled with domestic politics. On the whole, this condition was unfortunate for the overall relationship. Even worse, if bilateral trade tensions led to restrictions or sanctions against Korean imports by the United States, Korea's economy would have been put at considerable risk. As noted, this scenario was nearly played out five years ago.

Since then the Korean government has pursued a successful policy of trade diversification designed to reduce our export dependence on the United States and our import dependence on Japan. Of these twin objectives, the former has proved much easier to achieve. The U.S. share of Korean exports has gradually been reduced to less than 25 percent from 40 percent in 1980. This decrease has been accomplished by helping our businessmen explore new opportunities in nontraditional export markets such as Europe, the Middle East, Southeast Asia, China, and Latin America. At the same time, we have been opening up Korea's home market and encouraging U.S. companies to become more active in it. As a result, U.S. exports to Korea over the last few years have generally risen faster than Korean exports to the United States, and the two-way trade account is now relatively balanced.

Merchandise trade will doubtless continue to be the linchpin of Korea-U.S. economic relations. This is certainly one major element of continuity in Korea-U.S. relations. As for changes, the principal focus of change in the economic partnership is the development of a new trading scheme based on an emerging concept called an "industrial alliance."

The practical rationale behind the concept of an "industrial alliance" is quite simple and compelling. Korea's greatest industrial strength is its powerful manufacturing base. Our weakness lies in certain advanced-technology sectors in which we are not able to compete with the United States, Japan, and Europe. Conversely, America's strength lies in many of the same advanced technology areas where Korea is less competitive. Moreover, as the recent survey by the World Economic Forum seems to indicate, U.S. industry is actually lengthening its competitive lead in many of these areas. The challenge to American industry is to commercialize the fruits of its technological prowess.

I know that President Clinton is firmly committed to rebuilding America's manufacturing plants in those sectors where they have become badly rundown. I welcome this effort and wish it well; however, as an economist, I would have to caution against withdrawing resources from what the United States does best—namely, high technology—to rebuild or create manufacturing industries in which America is not likely to be very competitive.

In short, it would make better commercial and economic sense to combine U.S. high technology with Korea's manufacturing base in those sectors where such a partnership would be most competitive. This is what is meant by an "industrial alliance." To those businessmen who might object that Korea's labor costs are too high, I would respond that the United States could not forge this kind of partnership with a low-wage, low-skill economy. The prospective partner must have an economy sophisticated enough to absorb U.S. technology but not so advanced as to be able to compete with or replicate it. Korea is one of a very few countries that meets those requirements. Furthermore, Korean industry—unlike that of East Asia's other "little dragons"—is characterized by large-scale manufacturing units. These units are particularly well-suited to the type and scale of production that U.S. firms increasingly seek to relocate offshore.

In discussing this concept, I am engaging in both advocacy and prediction. U.S. companies are discovering the advantages of technology-based linkups with Korean firms all by themselves. For its part, the Korean government is trying to get the ball rolling by introducing a new program of foreign-investment incentives tailored to meet the needs of high-tech companies. New foreign investment on the approval basis was up 64 percent in the first half of this year compared with the same period last year. At least in part, this development is a vote of confidence by the international business community in the foreign investment and deregulation policies of President Kim's administration.

In fact, deregulation has been the centerpiece of the administration's new economic policy from day one. In the first year-and-a-half, hundreds of restrictive regulations, most dating from the 1960s and 1970s, have been abolished or radically amended. The President has pledged to continue his effort until the end of his five-year term. A good indication of renewed business confidence is the performance of the Korean stock market, which has risen more than 50 percent since President Kim took office last year after falling by a third in the previous four years. At the same time, the Korean economy, which grew at 5 to 6 percent last year—which was something of a disaster to us—is predicted to grow by 8.5 percent this year.

I have dwelt on the economic aspects of Korea-U.S. relations for basically two reasons. First, this is the broad area in which the United States and Korea interact with each other most directly and with the most profound and lasting effects. The end of the Cold War has by no means eliminated the need for strong political and military ties, but it has made it more apparent than even before that the future of our partnership will be largely shaped by the dynamics of economic cooperation. Second, economic change is almost always incremental. We can identify emerging trends and project them forward with at least some degree of accuracy. The economic future seldom comes upon us unannounced, whereas political events often take us by surprise and seem to form themselves into patterns and trends only in retrospect.

Few observers now doubt that under South Korean leadership, Korean reunification is inevitable. Moreover, it is likely to take place within our lifetime, probably within a few years. There are historical parallels of a sort, but no real precedent. The old East German state, for example, had the highest living standard, the most advanced technology in the Communist world, and its border with West Germany was almost porous in comparison with the so-called

89

Demilitarized Zone separating the two halves of Korea. Also, the German Democratic Republic (GDR) was never a one-man dictatorship; there was no "Great Leader" and no cult of personality. East Germany, with a population almost equal in size to that of North Korea, had only a third as many men under arms as the North has today. This brief comparison suggests that reunification when it does finally occur could present an even greater challenge than that which confronted Germany.

To meet that challenge successfully, Korea will need the support and understanding of our friends and economic partners—above all, the United States. I have no doubt that we will have it. Since the end of military rule in Korea in 1988 and the establishment of a fully civilian government last year, our two countries have moved closer together politically as we have come to share a similar political culture. This integration may not be so obvious on a daily basis, amid the cut-and-thrust of trade disputes and diplomatic maneuvering. Yet, over the long run, a common commitment to democracy provides the firmest foundation for good relations between nations, especially those of widely differing cultures and history.

Thus far, I have only referred briefly to the North Korean nuclear situation. The United States and North Korea have recently concluded another round of negotiations. A few words must be said about the nuclear situation on the Korean Peninsula. First, the International Atomic Energy Agency (IAEA) must secure transparency with respect to North Korea's past nuclear activities, including IAEA inspections of the two undeclared nuclear waste storage sites in Pyongyang. South Korea considers transparency of North Korea's past, present, and future nuclear activities to be essential to resolving the nuclear issue. During the negotiations in Geneva, the United States and North Korea agreed to conduct special inspections over a specified time frame.

Second, progress in the North-South dialogue is also essential to resolving the nuclear issue. The North Korean nuclear problem is as much an inter-Korean issue as it is a global, nonproliferation issue. Development of North-South relations must be pursued in conjunction with the negotiations between the United States and North Korea. In fact, the issue of a North-South dialogue is what held up recent talks between the United States and North Korea. Both South Korea and the United States wanted to include the essentials of a North-South dialogue, whereas North Korea wanted to take them out. In the end, North Korea accepted the details of the agreement.

Third, with respect to light-water reactor construction, South Korea looks forward to participating in a Korea-type, light-water reactor project. South Korea's provision of these light-water reactors to the North would greatly facilitate inter-Korean exchange and cooperation and would have long-term political implications for both South and North. Though not the perfect solution, South Korea's role in providing light-water reactor construction to the North would be an important factor in ensuring that the Korean Peninsula remains nuclear-free and that North Korea does not become a global merchant of nuclear weapons material. As we confront this latest challenge together, South Korea is confident that its broad and deep relationship with the United States—which has gone through both good times and bad—will stand us in good stead. We have come a long way since Percival Lowell concluded that "trade is not one of the mainsprings to action" for Koreans; but if that particular judgment was later invalidated, he was accurate in predicting a promising future for the Korea-U.S. relationship.

What began more than a century ago as a distant relationship between exotic strangers eventually has become a bulwark of collective security in East Asia and later a thriving economic partnership. With the passing of the Cold War, the nature of the security threat has changed—narrowing in scope while becoming more uncertain and potentially volatile. That threat, however, like the regime that sustains it, is a legacy of the past, not a harbinger of the future. The dawn of the 21st century will see the United States and a unified Korea joined in an industrial alliance that will set the tone for economic cooperation across the Pacific Rim.

QUESTION: What is the opinion of the South Korean government now that the negotiations have been completed between the United States and North Korea? Also, what are the relative strengths and capabilities of the North and South Korean armed forces? Public announcements by the U.S. government suggest that intervention in

South Korea by U.S. forces in the case of an invasion is a very high priority. In fact, some have rated it as high, if not a higher priority than protection of Kuwait. How much of a role are the South Korean armed forces prepared to perform should there be an invasion?

AMBASSADOR HAN: At every stage of the negotiations, South Korea was fully consulted by the U.S. government in Washington and also in Geneva. We dispatched the director general of the American Affairs Bureau to Geneva for consultation with Ambassador Gallucci. When the United States was negotiating with North Korea, negotiators came back to ask our opinions two or three times a day. Also, in Washington I was the main point of contact for the American government. When negotiations were concluded, there were people in both the United States and Korea who were unhappy about the content of the framework. Nevertheless, the South Korean government has officially come out in support of the framework. In negotiations, 100-percent satisfaction will not be achieved. Only in war can one win 100 percent of what one wants. In negotiations, one has to compromise and give something in return for things desired. On the whole, the tone of the agreed framework is good. The problem really is not the framework itself but how to implement the framework from now on. Thus, the next stage for the United States and South Korea is to see if North Korea will be in agreement with the proposed framework too.

As for your second question, South Korea has about 600,000 troops, whereas North Korea has almost a million or more soldiers across the DMZ. South Korea also has American soldiers on its side. Secretary of Defense Perry recently said in Korea that American troops would stay in Korea and that the troops are there not because of the nuclear threat but because of the threat from conventional forces. Nevertheless, if war were to come, the main responsibility of defending South Korea should rest on Korean rather than U.S. shoulders.

With respect to U.S. troops in Korea, the United States lost about 50,000 men during the Korean War in defense of Korean freedom; however, it should also be noted that when the United

States had a difficult time in Vietnam in the 1960s and 1970s, Korea was the only outside nation to send soldiers. South Korea sent 50,000 soldiers, and over 30,000 soldiers were either killed, injured, or missing in action. Hence, the bonds between the United States and Korea have been created and strengthened by more than just an economic relationship. It is more of a blood relationship, to a certain extent. Finally, American soldiers are in Korea not only to defend South Korea but also to guard present and future U.S. national interests. A U.S. presence in Korea guards the national interests of the United States, as well as those of South Korea.

One additional comment I would make is that South Korea's economy has been growing so fast that in ten years North Korea's economy will not be able to compete with South Korea's because the North Korean economy contracted by 50 percent over the last four years. North Korea may have many soldiers above the DMZ, but they will not be able to compete with South Korea in other areas.

QUESTION: Who is running North Korea? How do you see the relations between North and South Korea developing?

AMBASSADOR HAN: Experts agree that the future of both Koreas will be good again. President Clinton's letter to North Korea assuring the regime about the planned light-water reactors should help. Since 1973, Kim Il Sung's son, Kim Jong Il, has been groomed to succeed his father. Although he has not yet surfaced as the leader of North Korea, he will become the leader of North Korea in due course. Kim Jong Il has not yet been elected as general secretary of the party or president of North Korea. I believe he only has the title of Supreme Commander of Armed Forces.

On the other hand, there are several conflicting reports on the state of Kim Jong Il's health. Some people say he has diabetes and some people say he has had traffic accidents. The state of his health may mean that he will not be in power long, but at least in the short term, he appears to be the leader of North Korea.

The South-North relationship will be directly affected by whoever is the leader of North Korea in both the short run and the long run. If Kim continues to be the leader of North Korea ten

93

years from now, then a stable relationship between South and North Korea is possible. I hope through opening its doors, North Korea will have more contact with the South. This is the scenario we wish would happen.

There are two other scenarios. One is clearly undesirable and would be the product of North Korea's failing economy. The outside world hears stories that most North Koreans have only two meals a day and some have only one meal a day. The state of North Korea's economy prompts some to speculate about a Romanian type coup d'état or a sudden collapse of the North Korean regime. Such a development would be very problematic for South Korea because it may require South Korea to absorb North Korea. This scenario is one that South Korea does not want to happen, but if it does happen, South Korea will not emulate what West Germany has done to East Germany. We would like to manage the North Korean economy separately from the market economy system for some time. Very few North Koreans know what "price" really means or what "private property" means. These are the people who have been subject to central control and a socialistic system of economic management for so long that they do not know what price means. Things have always been rationed by the state to them. Hence, changing their ideas about the market system will take a long time.

Another scenario involves the transfer of power with collective leadership. For example, if Kim Jong Il should fall ill or have to step aside, some technocrats in conjunction with some military leaders may settle upon a system of more open collective leadership, which may open North Korea to the outside world. This would also be quite a reasonable alternative to South Korea; nevertheless, we would prefer the first scenario; that is, a strong leader who will force North Korea to open its doors to the outside world and thus lead the way toward a peaceful agreement with South Korea.

QUESTION: When I was in Korea in 1990, anti-Americanism appeared to be dying down, and it no longer seemed to be a significant movement. What is your assessment of the current state of anti-Americanism in South Korea?

AMBASSADOR HAN: I would agree that anti-Americanism is dying out rapidly in South Korea. Anti-Americanism flourished and reached its height in the 1980s because various authoritarians, people who wanted a dictatorial regime in Korea, were assumed to have been supported by the United States. As a result, those who fought for the promotion of democracy in Korea thought that the American government was behind the military in 1980.

But beginning in 1988 and particularly last year with the election of President Kim Young Sam, democracy has been fully established in Korea, and those who fought for the promotion of democracy now realize that the United States, in fact, supported their efforts in South Korea. There is no longer cause for people to become anti-American. If there are any anti-American views, they belong to a minority of young students who are sympathizers of North Korea, but even their numbers are decreasing rapidly. Now very few demonstrations against the American government or the United States occur in Korea. Eight or ten years ago, such demonstrations were a problem, but no longer.

COMMENT: An interview with President Kim Young Sam, published in the *New York Times* before the Geneva Agreement, created an impression among Americans that at least at that point, he was critical of the pace of U.S. negotiations with North Korea and felt that the United States was not taking a strong enough line. The interview also gave the impression that the government of the Republic of Korea viewed the North Korean regime as on its last legs, that collapse was imminent, and that the United States should take steps to bring about the collapse. All of this seems to contradict your earlier comments.

AMBASSADOR HAN: The article that appeared in the *New York Times* was not an interview. Rather, the article was based on a conversation between our president and the publisher of the *New York Times* who came to get advertisements from Korean businessmen in Korea. It so happened that the Tokyo bureau chief of the *New York Times* was also there, and it was he who wrote the story. A few days after the article, the president gave a full interview to the *Washington Post* and CNN, in which he expressed

95

his views on U.S.-Korean relations. These interviews were much more constructive than the one that appeared in the *New York Times*.

In any country, there will be at least two camps. Even in the United States you have conservatives and moderates. In Korea we have conservatives and moderates. When the negotiations are going smoothly to the satisfaction of moderates, the conservatives may be worried. Even after the agreed framework was published in the United States, many conservative Republican senators expressed concern about the content of the framework. In short, it was quite natural that some people would be concerned about the progress being made with North Korea at the time.

What President Kim really said was a warning to the United States. He implied that we South Koreans could draw upon a vast amount of experience with respect to dealing with North Korea. North Korea made many promises to the South Koreans. The basic agreement between South and North Korea and the Declaration of the Korean Peninsula simply became a piece of paper. North Korea never meant what they agreed to with us. In short, President Kim Young Sam's remarks were meant to caution the United States about North Korean negotiation tactics. He was only saying to the United States that it ought to strengthen its bargaining powers in Geneva. We should try to make use of what President Kim said to get more from North Korea.

The second point is that Kim Il Sung's death significantly changes the situation and hence calls for different negotiating tactics. At the time when the negotiations began, Kim Il Sung was alive. His death, however, meant a dramatic change in North Korea, and these facts have to be taken into consideration with respect to the negotiations.

QUESTION: What is the current state of Korea's economic relations with China, particularly southern China and Hong Kong? Do you foresee a stable China surpassing the United States as Korea's main trading partner within 20 to 30 years? Conversely, if the takeover of Hong Kong gets messy and Deng Xiaoping dies and is replaced by a more conservative leadership, will Beijing's relationship with Pyongyang backtrack a little?

AMBASSADOR HAN: According to the World Bank report, which estimated China's GNP based on purchasing power parity, China's economy was the third largest economy in the world last year. Some Japanese newspapers even estimated that the size of the Chinese economy last year was almost on par with that of Japan. If this is the case, China may even surpass it this year. In real terms, China's economy is on par with the Japanese economy, which is the second largest economy in the world. If China grows at the current rate of 10 percent for the next 20 years, China will become the largest economy in the world in 2020, even surpassing the United States. In that case, great opportunities exist not only for Korean traders, but for American businesses as well. Korea's bilateral relationship with China had been almost nonexistent until about four years ago; that is, until the normalization of South Korea's relations with China. During the last three years it has grown in leaps and bounds, and at the moment our total trade with China exceeds $10 million. As of last year, our bilateral trade with the United States was $36 billion. China's trade with South Korea has grown so fast that if this trend continues, China could eventually become the most important trade partner to Korea.

Regarding the relationship between Korea and China after 1997 when Hong Kong is returned to China, the preeminent financial position of Hong Kong may decline dramatically after 1997. Shanghai may replace Hong Kong. Indeed, Shanghai is likely to become an increasingly important financial center of East Asia, whereas Hong Kong is likely to lose its preeminent role there.

After Deng dies, there are several possible scenarios. Much depends on China's ability to maintain domestic stability, which in turn depends a great deal on China's ability to stabilize the relationship between its fast-growing provinces and slow-growing provinces. Without stability in China, there will be no stability on the Korean Peninsula, and this would be against the national interests not only of Korea but the United States as well.

Currently, South Korea is trying to expand its relationship with China to encompass more than trade. For example, during President Kim's recent visit to China, we agreed to a number of joint venture projects in several areas, such as the aircraft industry and switchboard system. In short, both government cooperation and private investment are taking place between China and Korea.

NARRATOR: Mr. Ambassador, thank you for this very informative discussion. I would also like to say a special word of thanks for the students that come to the University of Virginia from your country. They make a significant contribution, and we are most grateful.

CHAPTER SIX

U.S.-Chinese Relations and North Korea: Past and Future*

AMBASSADOR JAMES R. LILLEY

MR. LENG: It is my pleasure to introduce Ambassador James R. Lilley, whom I have known for many years. There is so much to say about Ambassador Lilley. He is currently the director of Asian Studies at the American Enterprise Institute in Washington, D.C. He was previously assistant secretary of defense from 1991 to 1993 and U.S. ambassador to China from 1989 to 1991 and thus was there during the Tiananmen crisis. Previous to that position, from 1986 to 1989 Mr. Lilley was ambassador to Korea.

Ambassador Lilley received his bachelor's degree and later his master's degree from George Washington University. He also studied classical Chinese at Hong Kong and Columbia universities.

He has served the U.S. government with distinction in various capacities. He worked in Washington with the National Intelligence Office, National Security Council, the Defense Department, and the State Department. He also served in a number of U.S. diplomatic missions in East Asia, including Thailand, the Philippines, Cambodia, Laos, Taiwan, and Beijing. It is my great pleasure to present Ambassador Lilley.

MR. LILLEY: The current dispute with North Korea is obviously critical. Nevertheless, my presentation will be mainly about China because if the United States can manage Chinese relations properly,

---

Presented in a Forum at the Miller Center of Public Affairs on 26 September 1994. Introduction by Professor Shao-chuan Leng.

Korean relations will shrink in importance. Talks regarding nuclear weapons are presently being held in Geneva, a topic that concerns all of us very deeply. There is a great deal of misunderstanding that I will try to eliminate about China's role in the North Korean equation. I have gone from fighting against the Chinese in Korea in 1952 to planning joint strategy on North Korea with them in 1990. It is important to understand how this transition in U.S.-Chinese relations has taken place and how the United States can manage it in the future, because that is the key ingredient in solving the North Korean problem.

At the risk of stating the obvious, China is a totalitarian country in the process of change. The past mistakes in China have been of cosmic proportions, and the costs have been very high. When Chairman Mao made a mistake in social engineering, 18 million people died. The Cultural Revolution killed numerous innocent people, and after Mao's death that era ended. The reforms of recent years are limited in scope. There are more questions than we can answer. American attitudes toward China have swung dramatically from euphoria in 1971 to disgust in 1989.

I had the privilege of being in Korea in June 1987 with the coming of democracy and in Beijing in 1989 when democracy was crushed. A reference to Charles Dickens' *Tale of Two Cities* is appropriate: "It was the best of times and the worst of times." In 1987 we saw the South Koreans facing many of the same problems the Chinese faced in 1989—an authoritarian, corrupt government, nepotism, lack of trust, and people in the streets fighting against it. The South Koreans brought about democracy, which still thrives today. The Chinese chose to crush democracy, but it has never completely died.

I arrived in China one month before the Tiananmen massacre of June 1989. When I arrived, several events were affecting China and influencing me. As I got off the plane in Beijing, I was surprised to be met by Taiwanese reporters in the middle of China, asking me what the United States would do about Shirley Kuo, the Taiwan finance minister who was attending the first Asian Development Bank meeting ever held in Beijing. Her attendance was an unprecedented step. Then there was the Gorbachev-Deng meeting, the great reunion of the huge Communist parties of the

Soviet Union and China in the middle of May. After the long struggles since their break in 1960, the parties were coming back together. The nightmare described by Alfred Mahan of the great Eurasian land masses joining together was perhaps being realized by this Gorbachev and Deng meeting. The third factor was the thousands of students in Tiananmen Square. Finally, I was confronted with a visit of U.S. naval ships to Shanghai in mid-May 1989. When the embassy briefed me on this visit, they said this step would keep the Russians and Chinese off balance because we were solidifying the Chinese-American military relationship while the Chinese and Russians were solidifying their Communist party relationship. This was sort of Kissingerian triangular diplomacy from the 1970s transferred to the late 1980s. Boy, were they ever wrong!

The Gorbachev-Deng meeting could hardly take place because of the thousands of students in the square. All of the talking heads of the American media were there—Dan Rather, Ted Koppel, and others—trying to cover the historic meeting of Deng and Gorbachev, but they saw that the real action was in Tiananmen Square. I rode a bicycle to the square and talked to the people there. I realized that something was happening of considerable import, but it was also increasingly obvious to me that the movement was going to have to be crushed. It had the inevitability of tragedy. I received orders from Washington to return home with the then-chairman of the National People's Congress, Wan Li, to assist in solidifying Chinese-American relations. This decision was dead wrong because the action was in China. The crisis was about to blow, so I told Washington I was staying, much to Washington's displeasure.

Since the Chinese military was going to be the instrument of the crackdown, we decided to withdraw the U.S. Navy ships that were paying an official visit in Shanghai as soon as possible in order to distance the United States from China's internal policies before the thing started to blow. As I was about to return to Beijing, I was watching television in the Shanghai airport and saw the premier, Li Peng, declare martial law. After he went off the screen, the music of "It's Only a Paper Moon" was heard. The Chinese in the television studio were mocking their premier in the last days of

101

press freedom before the crackdown came. It was defiance, and it was tragic.

The second defining event took place on the day after the Tiananmen massacre. Dissident astrophysicist Fang Lizhi, an activist who supported nonviolent means and was considered the spiritual godfather of dissent in China, came to the U.S. Embassy in Beijing and asked for refuge. He said he was on the most wanted list and would probably be executed. He asked us to protect him.

I had been asked earlier by a number of Americans to see Fang Lizhi and thus give the Chinese government a signal that the American ambassador supported human rights in China. During President Bush's first visit as President to the Far East in February 1989, Fang Lizhi was invited to a banquet at the U.S. Embassy in China, but the Chinese government prevented him from attending. There was a terrible flap in the press about this incident. This brave, clever, dedicated, manipulative man who had for years represented the intellectual dissent movement in China came to us asking for assistance, and we had no choice but to give him refuge. It took 13 months of negotiations before he was granted safe passage and allowed to leave China. Nonetheless, it was clear that despite our involvement with Fang Lizhi, the Chinese wanted better relations with America and were prepared to make concessions to obtain them. They wanted to punish dissidents as an example to other Chinese, but they couldn't touch Fang Lizhi. Various sorts of pressure—diplomatic pressure from Japan, Australia, New Zealand and Canada, and financial pressure achieved with loans from international financial institutions, the third yen loan package, and the subtle and indirect use of most-favored-nation (MFN) status—resulted in freedom for Fang Lizhi and amnesty for 800 others.

Still, you have to look at the Tiananmen event itself, the tragic inevitability of this Chinese morality play that was being acted out between the dissidents, the people supporting the dissidents, and the "heavies" in the leadership and their subordinates. Everyone was seeking the high moral ground. In my first meeting with Li Peng before the Tiananmen crackdown, I quoted a comment from Kingman Brewster, president of Yale during the student revolt in the 1960s. Brewster said, "If you lose your youth, there is no amount of crisis management that will make much difference in the long run." I quoted this to Li Peng, but I am not sure if it registered.

Ultimately, what drove the "angry old men" to seek revenge was the humiliation that the students inflicted on Deng's great moment of triumph with Gorbachev by successfully turning back the PLA by nonviolent means. These brave students humiliated the untrained country-bumpkin soldiers by talking to the troops and giving them water and food when they came to put down the students' rebellion. The leaders finally decided that such rebellious action could not be allowed, and in their anger, they reached for the gun. The message was that the system can't be changed by going outside of it.

What the old men had failed to appreciate was that since they had invited the world press into China to cover the Gorbachev-Deng summit, the press was also there to cover the crackdown at Tiananmen Square. The Chinese often muttered, "What's the big deal? In the Great Leap Forward, 16 million people may have died; hundreds of thousands died in the Cultural Revolution, and so what if 1,000 people get killed at Tiananmen?" The difference was the communications revolution. The whole world saw it and the Chinese dissembled about it. They were caught by the media and exposed, and they couldn't go back. However, they did return to their old techniques—close the door and beat the dog. The Chinese leadership wanted to drive the foreigners out and then take vengeance on the people who had challenged the regime by going outside the system.

What were the lines that went into Tiananmen? I mentioned the Great Proletarian Cultural Revolution between 1965 and 1975; the Great Leap Forward between 1958 and 1961; the social engineering that took place; the number of people who died of starvation because of Mao's experimentation with agriculture; and the harassment of so-called bad elements. Mao was convinced that this process of permanent revolution had to go on. Mao's ideas permeated the entire nation. One of the ironies is that the students in Tiananmen quoted him: "Bombard the headquarters; attack the center. It is time for change." Mao changed dynasties, and now the students wanted to change his dynasty. But Mao was no longer alive, and the man who replaced him did not view things the same way.

Deng saw that the solution lay in economic reform, and his planning of the 11th Party Congress in 1978 laid out the reform program in a careful and thoughtful way. Deng believed that economic reform should begin with agriculture, moving away from the collective and commune systems. Once an individual responsibility system was established in agriculture, funds begin to move from the countryside into the city, and there arose the more difficult problems of reorganizing industry, selling off state-owned enterprises, and moving into the free market. It was perestroika (economic restructuring) without glasnost (political openness).

With the rapid economic growth and unprecedented bumper harvests taking place in the 1980s, the three "nos" of economic policy—no foreign investment, no joint ventures, and no foreign exploitation of natural resources—changed. This reversal, however, was accompanied by inflation, corruption, and nepotism that was revealed blatantly in the habits of the top leaders, their children, and their flunkies. This sense of unfairness has always roiled the Chinese. The wise economic course fed political liberation, and certain magazines—the *World Economic Herald*, for example— appeared in Shanghai and began to criticize China. Moreover, Fang Lizhi criticized Deng by name, an unforgivable sin in China. Granted, it is true that hundreds of millions of Chinese were lifted out of poverty in the process of high economic growth and the introduction of foreign methods of material incentive. What also resulted, however, was ideological poverty. Finally, the death of former Secretary General Hu Yaobang, a reformer, on 15 April 1989 was the catalyst that triggered the fateful events.

After the crackdown, punishment by example began. Television coverage of the shaved heads of young people being dragged before the magistrates showed the Chinese people that if they revolted, mass imprisonment or death would result. Second, an unprecedented opportunity enabled the Chinese Stalinists to reassert socialism. They began the "retrenchment campaign" and attacked capitalism in the countryside by reducing credit to the most vital and productive village township enterprises and by reducing construction in the cities. These actions resulted in low growth, a burgeoning of the transient population, unemployment, unrest, and social deterioration. The old men who ran China stressed that the Chinese still lived by the four cardinal principles, which stressed political authoritarianism based on the ruler of the party, the proletariat dictatorship, Marxism-Leninism, and Mao Zedong Thought. This social contract would allow a degree of flexibility in the economic sphere in exchange for control of political thought. A great student fever resulted in a drive to leave China, which Deng sought to reverse. Also 100 million Chinese without steady jobs threatened the survival of the dynasty. In Manchuria, one million people in Harbin were transients who migrated into the city from the countryside looking for work as their village and township enterprises closed.

As I said, after 13 months of refuge in our embassy, Fang Lizhi left China. It was our job to see if we could then begin to rebuild our relationship with China on a more realistic basis. We did not want the rhetoric of the 1970s and 1980s, when the Chinese people were depicted as selflessly giving themselves over to the greater glory of China. Some Americans managed to distort consistently what was really happening in China.

Our efforts to rebuild the relationship with China were obstructed by a fractured American consensus. American perceptions of China had degenerated into partisan struggles and caricatures of the regime, resulting in an angry and feckless debate on whether to link human rights with MFN trading status. The people who called for such a linkage knew perfectly well (and are on record as saying) that it would not work. One cannot publicly humiliate China into making concessions imposed by the United States. This was tried but it didn't work, so the VSG had to reverse itself.

The amount of time presidential candidates spent employing purple prose and defaming each other about kowtowing to Communist dictators resulted in a severe setback to our China policy. I remember coming back from China in 1991 after we had bargained hard to put all of the building blocks in place only to find that we had a feeding frenzy of piranhas circling a dead body. I went to the Senate and found that their minds were fixed on the idea that the United States had to consistently and publicly punish China for its human rights violations.

We were trying to build U.S.-China relations on real issues: scientific and technological cooperation; protection for American intellectual property rights; a renewed education agreement that did not require us to send Chinese students back to China after they completed their studies; a mutual property arrangement worked out after four years of frustration; trade memoranda spelling out our understanding of market access; intellectual property rights; export goods made by prison labor; and the renewal of language programs with Johns Hopkins and Nanjing universities. All of these issues were bilateral building blocks that we worked out through hard bargaining. The terms were generally favorable to the United States because the Chinese wanted to maintain the relationship.

Later in 1990 when we saw the vulnerabilities in their system, we decided that the United States should take the initiative in setting the agenda for the bilateral relationship. Ever since the Nixon-Kissinger visits to China in 1971 and 1972, China had controlled the basic agenda—to wit, the relationship was predicated on common cause against the Soviet Union, Taiwan as an obstacle in Sino-American relations, and a U.S. obligation to participate in the modernization of China.

We turned this around, saying that there was a new agenda for the bilateral relationship, with the cornerstone being human rights. We also insisted that the United States must have a level playing field regarding trade, that China's markets must be open. We insisted that they must adhere to international standards on intellectual property rights and that they should not export products made from prison labor to us. Most important, China must agree to stop proliferating weapons of mass destruction—long-range missiles, nuclear weapons, chemical and biological weapons—to Third World countries such as Pakistan, Iran, Libya, and Syria. This was the focus of the renewed relationship we wanted, and China accepted it. We said to them, "We need you for international cooperation."

Keep in mind that this was just before Desert Storm. China was on the Security Council and we wanted them to work with us to sanction Saddam Hussein, even while we had sanctions on China in the wake of the killings at Tiananmen. China did so because it was in their own interest. Along with our allies, we also persuaded China to cooperate on finding a solution to the genocidal Cambodian civil war. The Cambodian problem remains, but we have at least come a long way from Pol Pot's earlier days when the Chinese fully backed him.

Finally, we needed China's cooperation on North Korea. In 1950, China had colluded in North Korea's attack on the South and later had inflicted a humiliating defeat on the United States in November of 1950. This was soon redressed by General Ridgway on the 38th parallel. Now, however, we wanted China to work with us in solving the Korean nuclear problem, and we succeeded in briefing the Chinese on the nature of the crisis. We showed them our information, and it was quite persuasive that North Korea was engaged in trying to build nuclear weapons. This was clearly not in China's interest. As China became involved and worked with us, we saw a number of things happen in 1991 and 1992. North Korea agreed for the first time to inspections of its nuclear facilities and gave us inventories of these facilities. North Korea agreed to joint entry of both North and South Korea into the United Nations and stood idly by while China recognized South Korea. The North Koreans also signed an unprecedented nonnuclear agreement with South Korea. This broke down in 1993 as we became embroiled with China over MFN and human rights.

China had found America to be an inconsistent supplier of military hardware and technology, and being realists, they had turned to other countries to satisfy their own national needs. It was disturbing to learn that all of the military items the United States would not sell to them they were now getting from Russia. Aside from medium-range Russian fighter bombers, the package deal probably included the technology for weapons of mass destruction, submarine propulsion, guidance systems on intermediate-range ballistic missiles, and aerial refueling.

It was clear that after we placed sanctions on our own military transfers, the Chinese had shifted to Russia, which was conducting a virtual fire sale. Russia was going broke and would sell any assets they possessed to anyone willing to purchase them. Even their technicians were for hire. Also, China became closer to Asian nations such as Singapore, Indonesia, Malaysia, and Thailand because these nations shared China's disapproval of American human rights policy. Those countries voted with China in Bangkok in March 1993 against the United States on human rights. China received further diplomatic recognition from Singapore, Indonesia, and Saudi Arabia as they moved ahead on the diplomatic front. The Chinese strategy was to keep a grip on internal politics while opening up to the outside world. They were successfully playing off the foreigners against each other. Because the British did not satisfy their demands in Hong Kong, China punished them using trade leverage. China also manipulated the United States on MFN by making deals with Germany and other countries at U.S. expense.

Future relations between the United States and China will be complex, and a number of points should be watched closely. First, watch what is called "horizontal pulls." The resurgence of regionalism has been dramatized by some as a return to warlordism and fragmentation of China, but this is not the case. Because of the lunatic policies of social engineering in years past—the Great Leap Forward and the Cultural Revolution—the regions don't trust the central government. The provinces are going to seek more economic autonomy and will be attracted to Taiwan and Hong Kong—rich, successful areas that are pumping investment into China while changing the face of South China. This process is moving ahead quickly and will have a great impact on the future of China. Hong Kong is the biggest investor, and Taiwan is second. Although some of these projects involve labor exploitation, the overall impact of thousands of small factories working for material incentives and successfully exporting is positive. Capitalism is a success, and competing on the world market is making China look good, but the central government often appears as an impediment to this process.

One has to realize that the scope of political differences within China is narrowing. In the old days, during the time of the Gang of Four and Deng in 1976, those who lost the struggle for power ended up dead, in reform labor camps, or in permanent imprisonment. The stakes were very high, and the differences were enormous: It was the capitalist role versus the socialist role. Those arguments have changed. The Chinese leadership today argues about inflation versus unemployment. It almost echoes the

108

arguments between Federal Reserve Chairman Alan Greenspan and the National Association of Manufacturers over whether or not to raise interest rates. The Chinese now argue about the nature, extent, and duration of subsidies to state-owned enterprises; tax rates; and inflation versus unemployment.

Further, the Chinese are going to decide their *own* course for the future, and it may not be ours. The Chinese formula for development is more inclined toward the Asian authoritarian structures such as those found in Singapore, in Taiwan under Chiang Ching-kuo in the 1970s, and in Korea under General Park Chung Hee in the 1960s and 1970s. The claim is that when dissent and strikes are eliminated, wages can be controlled, and a free-market economy can thus be successful. Open dialogue with political free-thinkers leads to chaos, on the other hand. Consequently, the Chinese are presenting their alternative formula: a free market in a large socialist "bird cage."

The Chinese approach challenges our own democratic principles of freedom of speech, freedom of assembly, freedom of the press, and emphasis on the individual. The Chinese stress that they have never accepted our cultural values and they don't accept them now. Neither is our system accepted in Singapore. The leaders of Singapore will hang a Dutchman and cane an American for breaking their rules. In China they will imprison their own people because it is their business, not ours. They argue that they have had major boosts in production and have lifted people out of poverty. Americans should focus on their own inner-city problems and not on China's.

China is making a disturbing push for military modernization. They are funneling extraordinary funds into their military and are not telling the truth about it. We have obtained their internal documents, and their goals are quite clear: They want the South China Sea and they want to control the sea lanes, the offshore oil, the fishery resources, and the territorial waters. Needless to say, this ambition challenges Japan, Southeast Asia, Taiwan, and Korea. China is, however, somewhat subtle about it. They will say that they want to be friends and will postpone the sovereignty issue, but it is quite clear that naval dominance is their objective. It comes with becoming a great power. A crisis over the South China Sea isn't necessarily going to take place, but certain people in the Chinese leadership, particularly the military, would like to have their way. Still, there are other people in the Chinese political structure who argue that China has enough internal problems without taking on the rest of the world. There is no need to get into a fight with the ASEAN nations and the United States. The United States in any case is not going to tolerate any interference in those sea lanes. There are many sensible and responsible people in China who probably will prevail in the long run and hopefully put this military genie back in the bottle. For now, however, the signs aren't very encouraging. The military buildup and dissembling continue.

The situation with Taiwan is somewhat different from that of Hong Kong, South China, and the Singapore area. Since its *de facto* political independence in 1949, Taiwan has been an extraordinarily successful country economically. Despite some rough edges, Taiwan is moving inexorably in the direction of genuine pluralistic democracy. The question for Americans is whether the United States can show preference to an enormous country like China, which is essential to our national interests even though it has a dictatorial government with Communist concepts, over a small free-market democracy like Taiwan. The question is, does Taiwan have to be punished to placate this Chinese ambition that claims a sovereign right to control Taiwan?

The United States is caught again and again in the middle of a moral, political, and economic dilemma by the Chinese insistence that this island belongs to them. We see the success that Taiwan has had, and at the same time we see the rise of the Taiwanese politicians who are pleading for international legitimacy. Taiwan has no seat in the United Nations. It doesn't have embassies in most countries, although there is the quasi-official "American Institute in Taiwan" in Taiwan as well as the Taipei Cultural Economic Representative Office in the United States that function somewhat as embassies.

I happened to be the second director of the American Institute in Taiwan for two-and-a-half years. The Institute is led by a director, not an ambassador. Even though it is not an embassy, it has many of the same functions. That is the way we play in this Chinese game. Taiwan has survived and prospered, but this has placed the United States in a delicate position. The United States must proceed carefully and let China and Taiwan work out their own intricate arrangements. At the same time, America must protect its democratic, economic, and political interests in both China and Taiwan, which are all intertwined. The outcome of these important decisions are part of the future and something with which we will have to live for a long time to come.

QUESTION: Could you please tell us more about the situation in North Korea?

MR. LILLEY: Briefly, the United States wants North Korea to give up their nuclear weapons program under total transparency and international verification measures, including access to their nuclear waste sites and whatever nuclear weapons and devices they might have hidden. The United States wants the entire program exposed.

QUESTION: What about delivery systems?

MR. LILLEY: That issue is important, but it is not front and center at the moment because their tests of ballistic missiles have not been very successful. Nonetheless, it would be rather daunting if Kim Jong Il possessed a handful of missiles that, even if inaccurate, were tipped with nuclear warheads. We must have access to the nuclear warheads first. North Korea has never adhered to the Missile Technology Control Regime (MTCR), although it has joined the Non-Proliferation Treaty (NPT). In terms of missiles, the United States has no legal right to bring sanctions or to pressure them. In the case of the nuclear weapons, we do have a legal basis because North Korea ratified the NPT and signed a safeguards agreement. It submitted to inspections and has given us some inventory of its so-called nuclear facilities.

The United States wants the North Koreans to live up to their NPT obligations, which should include verification and intrusive challenge inspections as a continuing follow-up. We want them to discontinue and dismantle the nuclear program, and we want the process to be peaceful. Additionally, the United States wants the Republic of Korea (ROK) to be in a leading role.

What the North Koreans want is to keep any nuclear weapons they may have. They want diplomatic recognition, foreign aid, trade, and investment under *their* conditions. They do not want "bourgeois liberalization" or "spiritual pollution" from us. North Korea is not impressed with China's special economic zones. Further, it wants to split the United States from South Korea and to downgrade the ROK. This conclusion stems in part from my personal experience in negotiating with them in January 1992. Essentially, North Korea wants to allow inspections only insofar as they do not reveal the nuclear weapons program. When the United States insisted on full disclosure and economic sanctions, North Korea threatened war. As a result, the United States backed off.

As a first step in resolving this dilemma, our advice is to take the war option off the table and deal with the nuclear issue through political, economic, and diplomatic means. The United States does not want to get into a situation such as the bloody war fought between 1950 and 1953. A prolonged conventional war would be more difficult for us than for them because they have complete control over their population. They have 1.2 million men under arms, 700,000 of whom are deployed south of Pyongyang up to the de-militarized zone (DMZ). There are also hardened sites for artillery and aircraft. The United States needs to tell the North Koreans that if they ever get involved in conventional war across the DMZ, that would be the end of them. North Koreans know about the devastating U.S. attacks on Saddam Hussein. They followed the Gulf War very closely. We do leave other options open.

The United States would be willing to give them much of what they want—aid, trade, recognition, and light-water reactors. Now, however, they are asking for considerably more. In Berlin the North Koreans not only demanded light-water reactors, but also conventional power for them in the interim period, to be financed by us, and they want us to compensate them for the rest of the nuclear facilities they have stopped building. In other words, the price tag goes beyond $4 billion up to the $5 to $7 billion range. Basically, it is a holdup. At this point North Korea is prepared to give the United States some of what we want, which is a cap on their nuclear program, an end to fuel reprocessing, the disposal of the spent fuel rods, and an investigation by the International Atomic Energy Agency (IAEA) inspectors, but they will not give us access to their secrets.

The major sticking point is that the North Koreans will not open up their system. The United States has said it will not proceed until they do so, but I see cracks in our position already, based on what I have heard from Geneva. Previously, the United States said that it was essential to gain access to nuclear waste sites so that North Korea's past nuclear program could be investigated and to see how much plutonium it had manufactured. The United States is now saying it does not have to do that for the indefinite future. The North Koreans have taken the position that the United States cannot inspect these sites because they are military installations. We know from aerial photography that they have stored their nuclear waste at those sites and built structures over them to conceal that fact. At this point there are areas where agreement can be found, and the United States has probably reached agreement with them in a number of areas where we know what they want and they know what we want. Nevertheless, there are still those sticking points that have not been solved.

The South Koreans are extremely nervous that the United States will cut them out of the deal and "grandfather" the North Korean nuclear weapons program. South Koreans argue that if that happens, proliferation will begin in Japan, South Korea, and Taiwan. Furthermore, the United States has no assurance that the North Koreans won't sell nuclear technology to Muammar Gadafi of Libya or Hafiz al-Assad of Syria; they have already sold scud missiles. Why wouldn't they sell them nuclear weapons, given the opportunity? Remember, nuclear weapons are small and can be transported aboard aircraft. It is going to be a tough negotiation, but there are three things on which the United States must stand firm. First, we must persuade them to discontinue and dismantle their nuclear weapons program. Second, this goal must be achieved without resorting to war. Third, constructive dialogue between the two Koreas is essential for long-term peace and stability on the peninsula.

QUESTION: Would you comment on the likelihood of reconciling the partisan political debate concerning China in the United States in light of your point that the future for U.S.-China relations is tied to a sophisticated, constant foreign policy?

MR. LILLEY: We have been concerned with that question for a long time. You may recall how the passions of the McCarthy period in the early 1950s ripped us apart on China. Some of that came back to become a bitter partisan issue in 1989. The good news is that the Clinton administration—and I will use a kind word—has shown "flexibility" in this case. They have moved from a strict principled position to a pragmatic position fairly easily. Most people breathed a sigh of relief when they extended China's MFN status without conditions in May 1994. Understandably, they had to go through some face-saving gyrations, but the beginnings of a consensus on China can now be seen. There are still some people in the United States who dislike China, particularly the more conservative politicians. There are also liberal politicians supported by human rights activists who find China distasteful for having suppressed democracy. In addition, there are people who have been ruined in disastrous trade ventures and have seen the worst side of the Chinese economy.

On the other hand, the prevailing tendency right now is the desire to become involved in and profit from the Chinese economic boom. The big American "houses" are excited about this prospect—perhaps too excited—and they are moving quickly into China. They see it as a market—30 nuclear plants being built in the next 30 years; infrastructure demands for railroads, airports, air control systems, aircraft—for all of the things that we in the United States do well. There is a tremendous demand for energy, an increasing need for pollution control devices, and a need for foreign capital and technology—the very things that we have. Furthermore, the Chinese are beginning to cooperate more constructively in the international arena, and we see signs that they are becoming more cooperative on the North Korean issue. They have upheld the U.N. embargo against Iraq. They are so far being constructive in Cambodia and are showing some inclination at least to have military talks dealing with the problem of strategic proliferation. It is perhaps the first step toward gaining an understanding with them and explaining to them how deeply disturbed the United States and its allies are about their weapons acquisitions from Russia and about their military intentions. The United States has been trying hard to encourage China into a dialogue with the Association of Southeast Asian Nations (ASEAN) on the South China Sea, and the Chinese did attend a meeting of the ASEAN Regional Forum (ARF) held in Bangkok in July. They weren't very helpful, but it was a beginning.

When China is faced with a decision about whether their interests are better served by international cooperation or by international defiance, if the choice is put to them clearly, they usually opt for cooperation. Certainly, it takes a great deal of diplomatic skill and work to present these options to them in a cogent way that will persuade them to make the decision we prefer. For the time being, President Clinton is off the petard on which he had hoisted himself and will eventually be making a trip to China. Secretary of Defense Perry will also go to China, and Secretary of Commerce Brown has been there already. The Chinese foreign minister will likewise be visiting the United States. We are starting a whole circus of summitry with China with all of the froufrou, folderol, and protocol that the Chinese love. We are putting a lot of energy into this effort, and there is a growing sense in the United States that we need to move beyond the economic field. I have had talks with John Deutch and other people in the Defense Department who feel that the United States must have strategic relations of some depth with China because stability, security, and prosperity cannot exist in Asia without it. As distasteful as some of China's political processes may be, the United States must make these deals as priority matters. Our priority should be a strategic partnership with China. That objective, matched with the money to be made from economic cooperation, makes for a fairly powerful package. If these prospective benefits can be articulated and sold, the United States can fashion an effective policy and start moving again. I hope, however, that the new policy will be without the hype of the 1970s and 1980s. Maybe this time the United States can accomplish its objectives while acknowledging the differences of opinion on human rights, Taiwan, and the South China Sea. If we can secure their cooperation, the whole regional system will be more stable and peaceful.

NARRATOR: Where does Japan fit in the China-Korea dynamic?

MR. LILLEY: I think Japan is a big player in both countries, especially in Korea. It boils down to remittances of currency by Korean residents in Japan, which have been estimated at anywhere between $300 million and $1.2 billion per year. They are essential to North Korean foreign exchange reserves, which in turn are used to buy supplies to feed their military ambitions. Were the Japanese to reduce these in conjunction with a Chinese reduction in shipments of oil, coking coal, and grains, the North Korean economy would be severely harmed. North Korea is almost an economic basket case already with declining GNP growth, power outages, and serious malnutrition. If Japan would agree to this strategy, I believe North Korea would quickly be persuaded to be more cooperative.

The Chinese still hold resentment against Japan, but they have admiration for Japan's economic and financial skills. Also, Japan is investing a great deal of money in China, particularly in infrastructure projects in northern China, telecommunications in the Yangtze Basin, and energy exploitation in the Northwest Basin, which are vital to the Chinese. When we were working to get China to make political concessions in 1990, Japan was a key player because it was willing to withhold the third yen loan package from China as long as China was on a collision course with the United States. The Chinese got the message. Our level of cooperation with Japan began to decrease after the Houston summit in 1990. Although Japan resumed its loans, it still retains substantial leverage over China.

It was interesting to note how desperate China was for this money in 1990 and how far they would go to get these long-term Japanese loans with low interest rates and interest-free periods. The package the Japanese had given them was very attractive. Japan is going to be a big player, but again, mutual resentments remain. Japan resents China's throwing business to the United States. China does not want the Japanese to have too much control. Also, the Japanese have to compete with Hong Kong, Taiwan, the United States, and Europe, and the Chinese find this multisided rivalry quite desirable.

NARRATOR: Thank you, Ambassador Lilley, for your truly illuminating presentation.

IV.

NORTH KOREA: THE COUNTRY AND THE NUCLEAR PROBLEM

CHAPTER SEVEN

North Korea's Nuclear Problem*

AMBASSADOR CHONG-HA YOO

NARRATOR: Robert Myers, who is president of the Carnegie Council on Ethics and International Affairs in New York, has had extensive service abroad in Asia. It is appropriate that Mr. Myers, to whom we are much indebted for this meeting, should introduce our speaker.

MR. MYERS: Ambassador Chong-Ha Yoo has had a long career in the Republic of Korea's foreign ministry. He began working there in 1959, a time well-chosen to begin one's career in the foreign ministry. As many will remember, after 1960 the community of states began to grow from 45 to 100, to 150, and now to 188 or more. As a result, several promotions to ambassadorships occurred in the foreign office of every country to accommodate all of the new countries, many of which had emerged with the end of colonialism.

Ambassador Yoo has served in Pakistan and in Africa and Europe. He was the vice foreign minister at a time when former President Roh Tae Woo and many others were trying to open the door to North Korea. Ambassador Yoo is one of the few South Koreans who has actually been to the North to negotiate an exchange of ministerial visits and he has played a key role in the reconciliation of North and South Korea. For that reason, I

Presented in a Forum at the Miller Center of Public Affairs on 2 December 1993.

suspect, he is now the Republic of Korea's ambassador to the United Nations, where many of those same battles still continue. Ambassador Yoo has also demonstrated his ability as a bureaucratic master in reorganizing government. He was able to roll over five different ministries and win the prize of the Korea Foundation, not only in the foreign ministry, but in a rather ingenious way of financing it. He is a man of many talents and much experience.

In the past, Ambassador Yoo has addressed in a very thorough way the problems in the Korean relationship and what the possibilities are for the future. We are happy to welcome him here today for a discussion of these issues.

AMBASSADOR YOO: My discussion today focuses particularly on North Korea's nuclear potential, a problem that has assumed an important place in the United Nations, diplomatic discussions, and Korean newspapers. About a third of the Korean newspapers are filled with articles on the nuclear issue. As exemplified by the press club statement and the resolutions issued by the U.N. Security Council and General Assembly, this issue is certainly serious. Somalia, Yugoslavia, and Haiti may be in the forefront now, but if current U.S. negotiations with North Korea do not go well and the matter is brought before the Security Council, then this problem is certain to overshadow all other issues. If the situation gets out of control, the kind of conflict that could erupt in Korea will be unmatched by any previous conflict, even those in Somalia or the former Yugoslavia.

Korea is a country that in many ways can be considered the ammunition warehouse of the world. The South has 43 million people, and the North has 23 million, for a total of 66 million people. Among that population, North Korea maintains a standing army of one million and has roughly one and a half million in total armed forces, including reserves. North Korea possesses huge military installations and hardware. Very few countries besides the United States and Russia can compete with the size of the military in North Korea. North Korea spends more than 20 percent of its GNP on military expenditures. Approximately one out of two healthy people older than 22 or 23 is engaged in the military in one way or another. The atmosphere is very heated.

Kim Il Sung has been in power since 1945—that is, for 48 years. Even if one considers only the period since he was formally inaugurated, he has been in control for 45 years. The reasons for his long reign of power are numerous, many of them unusual. Many diplomats from Russia, Eastern Europe, and China who have served in Pyongyang say there is no comparison to the kind of regimentation and isolation of a society that has occurred in North Korea. Some factors that have contributed to Kim's long reign of power are North Korea's militarization, social isolation, and idolatry of Kim Il Sung, making him a kind of demigod in the eyes of many North Koreans.

Alongside the idolatry of Kim Il Sung, an enormous amount of hatred has also been produced by the perceived threat of imperialistic powers, mainly the United States and Japan, which are believed to be falsely occupying South Korea. With support fostered for him by this hatred, Kim Il Sung is determined to liberate the South Koreans. The hatred toward Americans who are now in South Korea is frequently expressed through the use of extreme invectives and shouting. North Korea is a harsh and angry society. Currently, the eighth exchange of formal delegations between North and South Korea, four times headed by the prime minister, is occurring.

I visited North Korea two years ago for ten days with a group of 20 people. Twenty North Korean high public officials served as our guides. We weren't allowed to go everywhere, but if we insisted, they reluctantly had to agree. We visited many places and met many people. People in my group asked bold questions, and they answered with their typical answers. We discussed many things and talked heart-to-heart with some of the people. The group found that although the people felt that there was no political problem because no gap existed between the leader and the populace, they were at a loss with regard to the economy since the former Soviet Union had deserted them. China wanted everything paid in hard currency, and they had no hard currency. They admitted that they had an enormous economic problem and that they frequently discussed it. Their conclusion was that the only way to deal with the economic problem would be to reduce armament expenditures and direct more resources to economic development; however, given the "American threat," how could they reduce armaments? They felt that the best way to handle this threat was for the South Koreans to refuse the Americans and join with North Korea.

North Korea's poor economy gives the North Koreans a great incentive to build a nuclear bomb. North Korea is essentially a military society and needs to display its military strength before the people and outsiders to feel strong. As the economy becomes weak, it cannot compete with the South. North Korea began extracting plutonium in 1977 and has since officially admitted to the inspection team of IAEA (International Atomic Energy Agency) that it first extracted plutonium in 1989, but only 90 grams. IAEA teams have visited North Korea seven times under the agreement between IAEA and North Korea (which is a member of the Non-Proliferation Treaty), and according to its analysis, the IAEA suspects that North Korea has somewhere between 10 and 30 kilograms of plutonium. In addition, it has a good delivery system; in fact, North Korea is selling missiles to Iran and Syria. Recently, it successfully launched two missiles into the East Sea (the Sea of Japan), which naturally alarmed the Japanese. The missiles cover a distance of 600 kilometers, which would include the whole area of South Korea. If strengthened, the delivery range of their missiles could include the industrial part of Japan.

The South does not have information regarding the development of nuclear detonation devices because it is not subject to inspection. It is believed, generally, that the North is close to making bombs, although it is not known exactly how far the North Koreans have gone in the actual production of detonation and delivery technology.

A great deal of discrepancy exists between North Korea's declaration and the IAEA's findings. The IAEA wanted an accurate accounting of the plutonium and facilities used. North Korea, however, decided to stop IAEA inspections of special sites that the IAEA suspects are the deposit sites of the spent fuel and waste. The IAEA needs to see all of these sites to determine exactly how much plutonium has been produced. As a result, a confrontation erupted between IAEA and North Korea. North Korea has insisted that it will only resolve the matter through negotiations with the United States, not the IAEA or any U.N. organization. By its logic, the United States is the source of all threats to North Korea, and it therefore cannot agree to any solution unless the United States is a party to it. In the interest of resolving this matter and under the authority given to it by the Security Council resolution, the United States began negotiations, of which two rounds have been held. The third round will take place at a later date.

The first two rounds of negotiations went reasonably well. North Korea wanted the United States to make some reassurances that it would not threaten North Korea, to which the United States agreed. In the second round, the North Koreans said that the United States should pledge support of the North's plan to replace the current graphite system reactors with light-water systems, which would be a huge job. North Korea would need more than $1 billion to accomplish this conversion, and it would require a great deal of time. In the interest of development and reaching a solution, the United States has agreed in principle to support this idea. People in South Korea have also expressed their support and hope for the possibility of joining these negotiations. The graphite system is extremely unsafe—it is the same system that was used in the Chernobyl reactors—and is a technologically antiquated system whose use by South Korea's neighbor is extremely unsettling, to say the least. As a result, South Korea believes it would be beneficial for all concerned if North Korea were to change to a safe system. In the process of replacing the system, other issues of the North Korean problem can also be pursued further.

In the course of negotiations the North Koreans abruptly stopped and refused to admit any further IAEA teams to perform the regular inspections to which they had agreed previously. As of now, the cameras and the films placed in the North Korean nuclear facilities by the IAEA have run out, and as a consequence, the validity and continuity of the earlier inspections have been compromised.

If North Korea persists in its refusal and no further agreement is reached, the United States, the Security Council members, and all others concerned have indicated that the issue will have to be brought to the Security Council for some course of action. Such action would include cutting off the oil supply to North Korea and the supply of money from Japan. (Japan has a large Korean community in which many people are sympathetic to North Korea. Some of them have families in North Korea. A great deal of money is therefore being sent to North Korea, which has become an important source of foreign exchange revenue to North Korea.) If these issues are raised in the Security Council and some measure has to be taken in response, then tensions will escalate on the Korean Peninsula.

North Korea says that if the United Nations moves to initiate sanctions against it, North Korea will view such a move as tantamount to a declaration of war. It argues that since the United Nations is a party to the Korean Armistice of 1953 and the Security Council is a part of the United Nations, any hostile action on the part of the Security Council will be considered a hostile action on the part of the United Nations. If any such action occurs, then North Korea will be free from the obligation to observe the armistice agreement, which will lead to war.

Aside from the obvious rhetoric, there is also a level of seriousness to their interpretation and political stance. North Korea is very hard-pressed economically, and any further pressure in the supply of oil and money will severely cripple their industry, as well as their military. North Korea has more military hardware than South Korea. It has more than 1,000 aircraft, 26 submarines, 4,000 tanks, 4,000 armories, and more than 5,000 artillery units—a huge military establishment. If the supply of oil is discontinued, its absence would do a great deal of damage to the hardware. For example, tanks should be operated even during peacetime to keep up their maintenance. Sanctions on oil would be effective if needed, but if the North Koreans become too desperate, the kind of "no-win" situation that occurred in Waco, Texas, would be possible on the Korean Peninsula.

As a result, South Korea is trying hard to persuade North Korea to seek an agreement. Once the nuclear issues are resolved, then their relations with the South, the United States, and Japan will improve. If they normalize relations with Japan, they will receive quite a substantial amount of financial retribution from property claims. When South Korea normalized relations with Japan, it received about $500 million. But taking into account the passage of time and inflation, it is expected that North Korea will receive at least $5 billion from Japan once relations become normalized. North Korea, therefore, has much to gain by pursuing peace through a compromise with the outside world.

The political establishment of North Korea is very strange. Some within the military feel that any compromise with the West would be the equivalent of knuckling down to pressure from the enemy and the damage to its national prestige would be irreparable, resulting in a dismantling of its political and economic system. In short, the situation is delicate, and many important factors need to be brought out are hidden. The carrot-and-stick approach may apply here, but it is difficult to persuade the North Koreans and demonstrate what is good for them. The South is in the process of trying to achieve this goal and hopes that a catastrophic turn of events can be avoided; however, the South is not yet confident that this goal can be easily achieved.

NARRATOR: Your discussion of events on the Korean Peninsula is similar to an experience that happened approximately 5,000 years ago. Athens was the democratic trading nation, and Sparta was armed to the teeth. The stability was maintained in large part by other city-states, such as Corinth—a favorite topic of Chou En-lai—which would animate the balance of power and bring other nations to the side of the nation that was the weakest militarily. Within the region, is there any possibility of building up support and strength on the side of South Korea? Are there other Asian countries who might support the South's policies and serve as a counterweight to the military power of the North?

AMBASSADOR YOO: As of now, the numerical strength lies in the North, but states don't fight with only men and arms. The South has 600,000 well-trained and well-equipped armed forces. In addition, the U.S. armed forces, whose total actually exceeds that of a division, is also present. If an outbreak of war occurs, the South feels quite certain that North Korea will not have the upper hand.

Nevertheless, given that the population is indoctrinated and full of hatred, controlling North Korea will not be easy. If a war results in which the use of all hands is required, I do not think North Korea will be able to sustain the war for long. South Korea has a much stronger economy and greater overall military power. The South has the voluntary support of its people for its cause. There is virtually no sympathy among the population in the South toward the North, which was quite different 30 years ago. At that time, South Korea was less developed, and its political system was not uniformly supported. As a result, there was a great deal of sympathy for communism and North Korea in South Korea. With economic progress and the experience of political revolution, however, the people are happy and they now know more about North Korea. In short, if there is an outbreak of war, there is no doubt that the South can prevail over the North.

QUESTION: What role will China play in the resolution of this conflict? Given that China, of all of the Asian countries, should logically have the most influence on North Korea, what opportunity will China have to exercise its influence?

AMBASSADOR YOO: This concern is a logical consideration of South Korea, the United States, and Japan. South Korea has talked to the Chinese, and they completely agree with the idea that the international community should do everything possible to prevent North Korea from developing bombs. China's interest in resolving this issue is great because if North Korea develops bombs, people and governments in the southern Asian states will be greatly upset. Also, in Japan, more so than in South Korea, those of the right-wing will then be clamoring for nuclear armament, particularly since the North Koreans have been shooting missiles into the East Sea. North Korea's actions have aroused tremendous concern in Japan, but the possibility of nuclear armament gives China additional cause for concern. China is concerned that Japan might use the excuse of North Korean nuclear armaments as a justification for taking its own steps toward rearmament and/or nuclear armament. Such actions could prove to be a huge political and military burden to China; thus China, by all means, wants to stop North Korea from developing nuclear bombs. China is trying very hard to exercise its influence, but North Korea knows the Chinese position and also recognizes that the United States can use China as a lever (by manipulating China's MFN status) to put pressure on North Korea. As a result, the North Korean position has been to say to the Chinese, "We are thankful for your advice, but don't intervene. This matter is strictly between North Korea and the United States, and there is no place for you." China, not surprisingly, is very displeased as of now, and although the Chinese would like to contribute, the North Koreans have blocked access to them.

QUESTION: Have any of the North Korean diplomats been willing to come to conferences in other parts of the world? Do they make themselves available for discussion?

AMBASSADOR YOO: I would say no because North Korean diplomats are bureaucrats opposed to influences from the outside. North Korea makes every effort to be certain that its representatives do not deviate from the nation's stated policies. There are very few channels through which accurate information from the South can be transmitted to leaders of North Korea who are in the position to make decisions.

QUESTION: What is the known state of health of North Korea's leader, Kim Il Sung? If he were no longer in office, would his absence change North Korea's political stance?

AMBASSADOR YOO: Kim Il Sung had a large tumor removed. Intermittent reports stated that it was malignant, but so far he seems to be getting along well. Physically he seems fine. South Koreans believe that when he leaves office, problems will emerge.

QUESTION: A military treaty basically decided the metes and bounds of North and South Koreas on the 38th parallel. You have referred more than once to an existing attitude of intense hatred. Are there ethnic, religious, or social differences (aside from armaments and economics) generated over the line of demarcation as a result of this hatred? Are there elements of ethnic conflict on the Korean Peninsula similar to what one sees in other parts of the world?

AMBASSADOR YOO: There is no enduring ethnic or sociocultural factor that divides South and North Korea, although the ideological division of over 50 years has caused a significant split between the two. Korea was a homogenous country for at least 3,000 years of written history. According to some of the literature, the first kingdom was established 5,000 years ago. Thereafter, many kingdoms were formed and split, but there was no ethnic division among the people. Koreans all speak the same language and have the same religions—Buddhism, Christianity, and so on—although there is of course more Christianity in the South than in the North. Compared to the South, the North was historically a more open society because of the significant cultural influence from China. Thus, people in the North were traditionally more open-minded before the political division of the 1950s.

QUESTION: If no progress is made in resolving the nuclear arms issue, is it possible that a decision will be made to use force against North Korea? If so, what form will this force take and how long will the world wait before using force?

AMBASSADOR YOO: This question of whether or not to use force if all peaceful means fail is frequently asked. Koreans shudder when this discussion spreads to include questionable uses of force because such a topic is like dynamite in Korea. If a conflict develops into war even for a short period, the result will be catastrophic because North Korea has such a huge army with the capacity to fight for several months. The South is very vulnerable because of all of its industries, especially chemical, and more than ten nuclear generators, which are more or less open for missile attack. As a result of South Korea's vulnerability, the use of force should only be an option if North Korea initiates an attack on the South. The South should avoid any measure that could trigger any major outburst of conflict.

QUESTION: Regarding North Korea's low economic development, you mentioned that Japan was one of the major investors in the country. What other countries invest in North Korea? How does North Korea pay back these investments if its economy is so bad?

AMBASSADOR YOO: There is a great deal of discussion among the Korean businessmen in North Korea. South Korea invests a lot in neighboring countries. In Indonesia, for instance, South Korea has more than 3,300 factories, employing close to half a million people. In Sri Lanka, there are about 35 Korean factories. The South has also invested a great deal of money in China.

North Korea, despite all of the negative aspects, has a well-disciplined labor force with whom the South can easily communicate because no language problem exists. It has been suggested that instead of building factories outside of the peninsula, South Korea should build factories in the North. Many industrialists who originally come from North Korea want to invest in their native region. South Korea is, therefore, one state greatly interested in investing in North Korea.

Second, the South's interest also lies in the fact that it does not want North Korea to collapse suddenly due to economic and political difficulties, resulting in a huge outburst of refugees from the North coming to the South. South Korea should nurture and support North Korea for a long time until the people there are able to stand on their own.

The Chinese have also talked of investment, and Japan is very interested in investing in North Korea. Aside from South Korea and Japan, few countries are willing to invest in North Korea.

The political barriers should be lifted first, but North Korea, while eager to have investment and economic contact from the outside world, is also very fearful that through this economic contact, some "political virus" will be spread through the nation and undermine the system. Thus, it is caught in an ambiguous position.

QUESTION: Which part of North Korean society do you believe offers the best hope for a peaceful resolution; that is, which part of the society is best equipped to resist the dual problem of the adulation of Kim Il Sung and the hatred for the United States? Would it be the bureaucracy, the military leadership, the industrial leadership, or the intelligentsia? From which source could such a resolution arise?

AMBASSADOR YOO: First, clear information about how the internal policy mechanism works in North Korea is scarce. The North Korean negotiating team to the United States has outlined what it would like to do and has emphasized that many in North Korea support its ideas. At the same time, however, there are also hard-liners in North Korea who oppose them. The hard-liners are old and more imbued with revolutionary ideas; they are the old guard. Others are hard-liners because they have benefited from the system. Some people have concluded, for example, that the military is comprised of hard-liners because they fear that if the country moves toward more peaceful policies then the ways in which they benefit from the system will dwindle.

Perspectives differ according to a person's background and place in society. The people in the foreign ministry who have access to the outside world and outside changes have a relatively more realistic view. North Koreans trained in Eastern Europe, some of whom were sent as engineers to East Germany and Czechoslovakia, have a different view. People who are young and are technocrats are more realistic. People who are in the party hierarchy are afraid that their position will be endangered if things change. What is very ironic is that the son of Kim Il Sung, who is younger and represents to a certain extent the young generation, maintains a very hard line, while the older Kim is more diplomatic. This situation results in a strange contradiction. Some believe the younger Kim wants to show that he is a fighter and that he wants to establish his status by favoring a hard confrontation.

NARRATOR: One question that I imagine many people my age would ask is, "Was Korea worth it?" Dean Rusk used to say that the Koreans might never have had the chance for democracy that they had if there had not been resistance. He also said that today's younger leaders will emerge later into leading figures who can articulate very well the purposes and ideals of the country. Mr. Ambassador, you have confirmed Dean Rusk's statements. We appreciate your measured and insightful presentation.

CHAPTER EIGHT

North Korea and the United States: Promise or Peril?*

MARK P. BARRY

NARRATOR: President Kennedy said that domestic politics can hurt a president but foreign policy will kill him. For that reason, the Miller Center strives to provide a forum for as broad a spectrum of thinking about critical foreign policy issues as possible. The Miller Center is not an advocacy body but it tries to study and look at various points of view. That is a core principle in its philosophy. The Miller Center is a place where people have learned how to handle different points of view with a kind of civility for which the University of Virginia is famous.

Mark Barry is a graduate student approaching the end of his studies. His academic career here has been quite distinguished. He is one of a handful of Americans who met North Korean President Kim Il Sung in April 1994, and he has visited North Korea twice. His dissertation is a broad historical study narrowly focused on American relations with North Korea from 1987 to 1994.

Mr. Barry received his bachelor's degree *summa cum laude* from Arizona State University and his master's degree in national security studies from Georgetown. He helped arrange two roundtable conferences of experts and policymakers on the North Korean nuclear issue chaired by Admiral William J. Crowe, former

---

Presented in a Forum at the Miller Center of Public Affairs on 7 July 1994.

chairman of the Joint Chiefs and now ambassador to the Court of St. James. Mr. Barry is a member of the Academy of Political Science, the World Affairs Council of Washington, D.C., and the Asia Society. He is currently director of research at the Summit Council for World Peace in Washington, D.C., while completing his doctoral program at the University of Virginia.

MR. BARRY: When I first decided on the topic of the United States' relations with North Korea, I was concerned that I would not have enough material for a dissertation. Back in 1990, not much was said about U.S. relations with North Korea. It was a very static relationship frozen by the armistice agreement of 1953. As it turned out, this topic became a moving target, especially since 1992, as the nuclear issue became prominent. I decided, however, to remain true to my original intent of research on U.S. relations with North Korea because even though the nuclear issue is certainly a crisis that needs to be solved and an overarching development in U.S. relations with North Korea, it is not the defining element.

North Korea and the United States operate very much on a "perceptual" level. Between them are the problems of hatreds, resentments, and fears. These feelings are deeply entrenched on both sides, and also on the South Korean side. In April, when I returned from Pyongyang through Beijing and back to Seoul, I found that attitudes in South Korea toward the North were very harsh and extreme. It is almost impossible sometimes to conceive of the two Koreas having bilateral discussions without some intermediary. Because of this situation, President Jimmy Carter's successful efforts to defuse the nuclear issue through his meetings with Kim Il Sung and his role in conveying the North Korean leader's summit invitation to South Korea's President Kim Young Sam were very helpful. This approach showed that the United States was able to play, however unwittingly, an intermediary role.

For the sake of overall balance, I would like to present what I perceive to be the North Korean view, a view seldom covered in the media. Americans may not agree with how North Koreans feel, but their feelings are nonetheless strongly held and at least deserve a hearing.

North Koreans harbor a very deep grudge against the United States for two main reasons: the division of Korea and the American occupation of the southern part of Korea from 1945 to 1948. The United States had good reasons for pursuing the course it did, but from the North Korean point of view it is a source of tension and aggravation. Probably the strongest feelings of North Korean ill will toward the United States, something not always understood by Americans, are due to the fighting of the Korean War. Because of U.S. air superiority in the war, North Korea suffered tremendous conventional and napalm bombing to the point where the capital city of Pyongyang and most other major cities and industries were destroyed. Although South Korea also suffered great devastation, the North, from an objective standpoint, probably suffered more.

North Korea resents other American actions taken since 1953. North Koreans resent the mutual security agreement with South Korea and the maintenance of 36,000 American troops in South Korea. North Korea also perceives that the United States controls both visible and invisible barriers to North Korea having normal diplomatic and economic relations with the industrialized world (the United States, Western Europe, and Japan). Americans also tend to forget that the United States is still technically at war with North Korea. The armistice that ended the fighting in 1953 is still in effect. Presently, the Military Armistice Commission (MAC) supervises the armistice, and North Korea has recently been vociferously arguing that the MAC be replaced by a peace treaty. This request is not new on North Korea's part, but it is one that needs to be reexamined if major improvement is to occur in U.S. relations with the North. A normalization of diplomatic relations certainly cannot occur without a peace treaty. From the end of the Korean War until the late 1980s, the only significant contact the United States had with North Korea was at the Geneva Conference in 1954. At that time, the North simply took the same position as the Chinese and the Soviets, so absolutely no progress was made.

U.S. policy through approximately 1987 was to avoid Pyongyang. The United States simply supported the position of the South on all matters. In 1983 under President Reagan, the United States attempted to arrange informal conversations in neutral settings between American and North Korean diplomats. This initiative was cut short when North Korea blew up much of the South Korean cabinet during an official visit to Rangoon, Burma.

In 1987, Assistant Secretary of State for East Asian and Pacific Affairs Gaston Sigur took a bold step, undoubtedly with the support of Secretary of State George Shultz and with a great deal of encouragement, I believe, from the Chinese. Assistant Secretary Sigur gave a speech to the Foreign Policy Association in New York that was mildly conciliatory toward North Korea. The speech was significant because for the first time, an American official called the North by its official name, the Democratic People's Republic of Korea (DPRK). Assistant Secretary Sigur extended a U.S. hand in the hope of finding a way to come to terms with North Korea. It was a very promising speech. This overture was certainly made with the 1988 Seoul Olympics in mind. Unfortunately, four months later, the North blew up a Korean Airlines plane flying over the Indian Ocean, killing about 150 people. Nonetheless, the Seoul Olympics were held without incident. Again in late 1988, the United States allowed American diplomats to have informal contact with North Korean diplomats. An important step forward took place in December of that year when for the first time, diplomats representing Washington and Pyongyang met in a Beijing hotel for a round of conversations. Since that time through May 1993, 33 such dialogues have occurred in Beijing. At first, the dialogue seemed promising, but after the first two or three meetings they became rather scripted. None of the diplomats were empowered to take any initiative. These meetings were merely a point of contact and a means of exchanging positions. Neither side learned very much about each other. Many argue that this dialogue should have been raised to a higher level long ago.

I want to point out for the sake of historical comparison that from 1955 until President Nixon's 1972 trip to China, approximately 150 meetings were held in Warsaw between the American and Chinese ambassadors to Poland known as the Warsaw Talks. These meetings represented an important dialogue. In particular, they were very useful in helping the United States and China understand each other's position over the Vietnam War. For this reason, some scholars wonder why the United States did not try to upgrade the dialogue with North Korea earlier. Although the United States had been aware since the early 1980s through overhead (satellite) surveillance of the developments at the Yongbyon research facility 60 kilometers north of Pyongyang, the United States did not publicly admit its concerns about North Korea's nuclear capability until late 1989 and early 1990. When asked about this situation by reporters, the official U.S. position was that North Korea had joined the Non-Proliferation Treaty in 1985 and it had 18 months to sign a safeguards accord. It had not done so in that time, and the International Atomic Energy Agency (IAEA) and the United States were still waiting for it to comply. Once North Korea was in full compliance, the United States would be much more satisfied. In 1990, at a congressional hearing, the State Department listed five areas where positive actions by North Korea would encourage further steps by the United States. It is interesting to contrast these five points with the situation in 1994. First, the United States wanted progress in North-South dialogue. Second, it expected North Korea to conclude and implement the IAEA safeguards accord. Third, the United States wanted unambiguous North Korean assurances against state terrorism. Fourth, the United States was looking for some sort of confidence-building measures. Finally, the United States wanted to establish a process to return remains of over 8,000 Korean War MIAs over and above those returned in 1953-54.

As it turned out, 1990 and 1991 were very momentous years for the Korean Peninsula. A sudden meeting was held in San Francisco in June between South Korean President Roh Tae Woo and Soviet President Gorbachev. In September 1990, the first prime ministerial level dialogue between North Korea and South Korea occurred. This dialogue was the first of six that would take place over the next two years. Likewise, Japan suddenly began to open up a dialogue with North Korea, and the Soviet Union established diplomatic relations with South Korea at the end of September 1990. Finally, the United States unilaterally withdrew about 4,000 troops from South Korea as part of President Bush's plan to slowly and carefully reduce American forces in South Korea. In 1991, an important American decision was made: The United

States decided to remove all land-based (and later air-based) tactical nuclear weapons from overseas bases. This decision was not taken for the sake of the Korean Peninsula alone; it had much more to do with seeking reciprocity from the Soviet Union. By the end of the year, President Roh Tae Woo declared there were no nuclear weapons in South Korea. On the negative side, 1991 was also the year of the Soviet decision to end the sale of oil and other goods to North Korea at so-called friendship prices. This decision had a very damaging impact on the North Korean economy. Finally, 1991 ended on an upbeat note, with two historic agreements between North and South Korea—one on nonaggression and exchanges and the other on denuclearization.

In recognition of this progress, President Bush, while visiting Seoul in January 1992, decided with President Roh Tae Woo to cancel that year's Team Spirit, the annual joint U.S.-South Korean military exercise. That was the only time to date that a Team Spirit exercise was canceled. The United States also granted a one-time, high-level meeting in New York between Kim Yong Sun, North Korea's third-ranking official on foreign policy after President Kim Il Sung and his son, Kim Jong Il, and U.S. Undersecretary of State for Political Affairs Arnold Kanter. The United States viewed this move purely as an informational meeting with an authoritative level of North Korean leadership, held both to convey U.S. concerns about the North Korean nuclear program as well as to indicate that a better relationship lay ahead if North Korea were to abide by its nuclear commitments. Finally, by late spring of 1992, the director general of the IAEA, Hans Blix, arrived in Pyongyang after North Korea had finally signed and ratified the safeguards accord. Blix was able to visit the Yongbyon facilities and see for himself what the DPRK nuclear program was like. Subsequent to his visit, the first of six ad hoc IAEA inspections took place.

In the interim, the United States continued to maintain a skeptical, if not suspicious, posture toward North Korea as a result of its interpretation of intelligence data. To this day there is no clear consensus in the administration and among the intelligence agencies about the precise nature of the North Korean nuclear program. About the only thing agreed upon is that North Korea reprocessed more plutonium than it admitted. Too many "ifs" remain to conclude that the North Koreans have a nuclear weapon at this point.

Though perhaps unintentionally, this U.S. posture in 1992 toward North Korea's nuclear program had a dampening effect on the possibilities for improvement in North-South Korean and Japanese-North Korean relations. So much momentum came from the two inter-Korean agreements that President Roh Tae Woo strongly desired to have a North-South Korean summit meeting. U.S. pressure was applied to the South Koreans to slow inter-Korean momentum by insisting that the nuclear issue had to be resolved before a summit could take place. Similarly, the Japanese probably would have been able to make progress in their efforts to establish diplomatic relations with North Korea, but the dialogue between the Japanese and the North Koreans was ultimately abandoned due to the unresolved nuclear issue.

Admittedly, North Korea never suspected that the IAEA was so shrewd or so technically capable of detecting the true history of their program—at least to the extent that it did. North Korea certainly deceived and, to some extent, lied to the outside world about the nature of its program. The question is: Did it do so to hide a weapons program or protect a bargaining chip with ambiguity? At the same time, there is disagreement as to whether North Korea is technically capable of fabricating, delivering, and detonating a nuclear weapon. An internal Chinese document recently obtained by the Western press states that in China's judgment, the North Koreans are still at too primitive a stage technologically to develop a nuclear weapon. This statement may help account for the Chinese position preferring negotiations and dialogue to sanctions.

Tensions began to increase from September to October 1992. No progress was made in negotiations for mutual North-South Korean inspections. They could not come to any precise agreement on a procedure. In the meantime, with South Korean presidential elections set for December 1992, the South uncovered in October a North Korean spy ring allegedly including a secretary to leading opposition candidate Kim Dae Jung. The timing of this incident was intended to sour the atmosphere between the two Koreas. Despite the fact that regular IAEA inspections were occurring, there was a lack of North-South Korean progress, and U.S. suspicions about North Korea's nuclear plans increased. In this atmosphere, the United States and South Korea announced that they would hold the Team Spirit exercises in 1993. At that moment, North Korea went ballistic. The ninth prime minister's dialogue scheduled for December 1992 was unilaterally canceled by North Korea.

Moreover, the IAEA was emboldened. The IAEA's analysis, going back to 1989, indicated that more plutonium was reprocessed than the North Koreans admitted. It has been reported that North Korea's five-megawatt (elective) reactor was shut down for 100 days in 1989. It was supposedly at this time that North Korea could have reprocessed enough plutonium for one or two nuclear weapons. CIA Director Woolsey publicly testified to this information, although the CIA later revised that estimate downward. The evidence now indicates that the reactor was shut down for no more than 75 days, yielding enough plutonium for no more than one nuclear weapon, yet still more plutonium than North Korea had admitted. Furthermore, the United States had satellite evidence that North Korea had taken two nuclear waste disposal sites, bulldozed over them with earth, planted two buildings on top, put in some artillery pieces and jeeps, called them military facilities, and told the IAEA they could not inspect these sites because military sites are not covered by the NPT.

By early 1993 the IAEA demanded that North Korea submit to special inspections—something that had never been asked of any NPT signatory. North Korea refused. Finally, at an IAEA board of governors meeting, IAEA officials produced before-and-after photos of the waste dump sites with the buildings on top of them. These photos, which were provided by the U.S. government, made the deception very clear. On that basis, the IAEA board of governors asked North Korea to comply forthwith; otherwise, this problem would have to be brought to the attention of the U.N. Security Council. Two weeks later, North Korea took the bold step of announcing its intention to withdraw from the NPT. According to the provisions of the NPT, this withdrawal was allowed, but all 150 signatories to the NPT had to be notified and a 90-day period had to elapse before the withdrawal would take effect. Suddenly, a crisis emerged. The United States, in particular, felt the sense of crisis because no other nation feels more strongly about the NPT and nonproliferation than the United States does. Furthermore, with the NPT up for renewal in the spring of 1995, there was a very strong feeling that the sanctity of the NPT had to be preserved, and therefore North Korea somehow had to be made to comply.

The desire to preserve the NPT created a new situation. The United States, as a result, was finally persuaded to begin some sort of high-level dialogue with North Korea. The initial willingness of the Seoul government to encourage the United States to establish a bilateral, high-level dialogue with North Korea is another factor that made this situation different. It had been the past position of previous South Korean governments to oppose bilateral U.S.-DPRK dialogue. South Korea was afraid that North Korea would then use the South's absence as leverage against it by trying to cut a deal directly with the United States. The position of South Korea at the outset of this crisis was positive and encouraging. It is unlikely that the United States would have gone forward without South Korean support, although the ROK was soon to have second thoughts.

Since both Koreas were admitted as full members to the United Nations in September 1991, a North Korean mission to the United Nations with a fully accredited ambassador now existed. Thus, in early 1993 the United States began communicating with North Korea in New York, rather than in Beijing. American and North Korean working-level diplomats held talks in a basement room in the Secretariat building. The level of contact was never higher than the U.S. deputy assistant secretary level. In the beginning the talks were informal, but they became increasingly formal, particularly later that year. Each side would convey its position to the other, and then each side would wait for the promised response, usually conveyed by fax, to its position. In fact, much of the dialogue between North Korea and the United States has been conducted by fax. Even that level indicates progress. In the past if a State Department official received a call from the DPRK U.N. mission, the U.S. official was not allowed to accept the call.

Based on that initial contact at the United Nations, two rounds of official high-level U.S.-North Korean dialogue occurred, led by

141

Robert Gallucci, assistant secretary of state for political-military affairs (late ambassador-at-large), and his North Korean counterpart, Kang Sok-Ju, the first vice foreign minister. The first round of the dialogue was held in June 1993 in New York. At the eleventh hour, literally the evening of the day before the North Korean withdrawal from the NPT was to have taken effect, North Korea suspended its withdrawal from the NPT "for as long as necessary." That was a major accomplishment. It was also agreed that the dialogue should continue.

The second round was held in July 1993 in Geneva. North Korea asked the United States if it could provide directly or indirectly for "light-water reactors." These modern reactors produce far less plutonium than the Soviet-made graphite moderator reactors the North now has and require imported fuel. This request was at first regarded by the State Department as unusual, but at the end of the second round of dialogue, the U.S. position was to take a positive attitude toward it. It was agreed that a third round of negotiations would be held in September if the DPRK made progress in dialogue with South Korea and if it allowed the IAEA to continue to conduct inspections to ensure continuity of safeguards.

The real nature of the problem finally came out in August and September 1993. North Korea has a problem dealing with the IAEA because it is offended by the IAEA's legalistic and almost strident approach. The IAEA points to various provisions in the NPT and essentially says that since North Korea signed the treaty, it is obligated to do a number of things. The IAEA became more aggressive after its failure in Iraq, but the North resents its intrusiveness, which it claims goes beyond stated procedures.

On the other hand, the primary goal for North Korea is a breakthrough with the United States. Some argue that North Korea is merely using its nuclear program as a card by which to extract concessions from the United States. That evaluation is partly, but not completely, true. Political and economic concessions are indeed important, but even more important for the North is obtaining legitimacy through U.S. recognition. The North Koreans hunger for respect and acceptance as equals from the rest of the world, but on their terms. The potential threat of nuclear weapons (not their

142

Mark P. Barry

actual use) has value, but North Korean leaders also realize that they cannot feed people with nuclear weapons. They cannot reverse a stagnant economy with negative growth with nuclear weapons. I disagree with those who argue that DPRK nuclear weapons would be sold to Libya, Iraq, and Iran; money from such sales alone could never revive the North Korean economy.

The United States began to realize that a significantly greater carrot had to be offered to North Korea in order to break the deadlock on the nuclear issue. The North has been arguing since summer 1993 that a package deal could solve the nuclear issue. A thousand references have been made in the North Korean press over the last year asking for a package deal. Every North Korean ambassador has been stating to the local press that this type of deal is what North Korea wants and that a package deal should be built on simultaneity, not with U.S. preconditions.

The United States finally devised an unspecified package deal in early November 1993. Presumably it included the light-water reactors and some sort of road map leading toward full diplomatic relations. On 23 November 1993, however, South Korean President Kim Young Sam made his first official visit to Washington. He was very upset with this U.S. package deal despite the intimate involvement of his foreign minister because he worried that back home his government would appear to be on the sidelines. President Kim quashed the deal. Instead of it being called a "comprehensive approach," as President Clinton referred to it, it was renamed the "Broad and Thorough" approach. The "Broad and Thorough" approach was simply an indication of what might come and was not presented to the North at this time. One could conclude that the South Koreans have actually been running hot and cold in terms of their support of the United States in negotiations with North Korea. As a result, many more meetings had to be held at the United Nations as well as much wrangling with the IAEA because of U.S.-ROK avoidance of a political or package deal approach. Meanwhile, IAEA inspectors were finally allowed into North Korea in March 1994, but they were not allowed to do a complete inspection. The North held out, preventing a full inspection until May 1994.

Another, more serious crisis emerged when North Korea announced its intention to defuel and refuel its main reactor in May. The spent fuel was enough to produce four or five nuclear bombs. This process was one the IAEA wanted to observe, supervise, and sample in its own way. The IAEA inspectors on the ground at the facility made an agreement with the North Koreans stating that "we prefer to do it our way, but if you want to do it your way, we would accept it." IAEA officials in Vienna, however, quickly overruled their inspectors, thus creating a tremendously tense situation. North Korea was unnerved, and it became more hostile. This reaction may or may not be evidence that there are contending forces in North Korea—hard-liners and moderates that are vying over how to handle the nuclear issue. To some extent this is probably the case. The episode also indicates that all too often the United States has encouraged the IAEA to negotiate with North Korea alone, out of regard for the agency's independent authority. But the North Korean-IAEA relationship—like a cat and dog alone in a room—is so conflictual that U.S. aloofness has been detrimental. In the end, a terribly contentious situation arose in which North Korea withdrew the fuel rods at unprecedented speed. Even though the IAEA inspectors were allowed to watch the process, they were not able to conduct the tagging and sampling of the fuel rods in the manner in which the IAEA would have preferred. Thus, a situation was created in which the IAEA in many ways simply gave up and complained to the U.N. Security Council. On 2 June the United States announced that it would begin to consult with its allies and other members of the Security Council about invoking sanctions on North Korea.

Soon thereafter, President Jimmy Carter made his trip to North Korea. He was quite aware of the differences within the administration over the nuclear issue. Carter opposed the march toward sanctions; he believed that path would lead to war. He avoided speaking about the matter with Secretary Christopher, whom he had twice approached in the past about visiting North Korea and who asked him twice not to go. This time Carter contacted Vice President Gore, who encouraged the trip. Gore broached the subject with President Clinton just before Clinton left for the D-Day ceremonies in Normandy. President Clinton said he would be happy for Carter to go on the condition that he go as a private citizen, not as a special envoy of the United States carrying any formal message from the President.

The result of President Carter's trip was that the North Koreans confirmed an offer made a week earlier to Selig Harrison of the Carnegie Endowment: The DPRK would freeze its nuclear program in exchange for U.S. provision of light-water reactors. They confirmed this offer in writing in a document signed by the first vice foreign minister. On that basis and that basis only, the United States agreed to hold the third round of talks with North Korea in July 1994. President Carter succeeded in turning around a dangerous situation. I have been told very forthrightly by my North Korean contacts that had President Carter not gone to North Korea or had his visit not succeeded and sanctions were invoked, it would have led to war within a matter of weeks. North Korea has unambiguously stated that the imposition of any sanctions whatsoever by the U.N. Security Council would lead to a declaration of war. This word came from senior North Korean officials, not bureaucrats simply trying to stir up some commotion.

Diplomacy and negotiations have to be tried because war is not an option. War is a last resort. As dangerous as North Korea's development of nuclear weapons would be, pressing it with increasingly tight economic sanctions will actually create the very situation the United States is trying to avoid. The nonproliferation objective is to avoid a nuclear arms race among the two Koreas, Japan, and China. The irony is that pressing for sanctions, with North Korea as obstinate as it is, is exactly the kind of policy that will bring about this scenario. Considerable evidence exists to support trying other policy options. President Carter's visit proves that sending a senior American emissary for direct dialogue with Kim Il Sung, the source of DPRK policy, can be effective. I have been personally involved in private efforts to persuade President Nixon, President Carter, and former Joint Chiefs of Staff chairman Admiral Crowe to go to North Korea. All of them felt constrained by the Clinton administration, which felt that the situation was not right for them to go. It is surprising, for example, that even the initial high-level dialogue that began in June 1993 was only at the assistant secretary level. Initially, it was expected that Undersecretary of State for Political Affairs Peter Tarnoff would have been the one to commence the high-level dialogue with North Korea. North Koreans feel there has been a tremendous lack of respect, decorum, and trust from the United States. This desire for respect is the key.

President Carter said he is not a North Korean expert, but he could sense that the North Koreans were craving this kind of American recognition. Americans do not have to accept their social system. The United States never accepted the Chinese social system when President Nixon traveled there in 1972 and when President Carter established official diplomatic relations in 1979. The North Koreans are perhaps the proudest people on earth. It is said that even if they are starving, they will tighten their belts and take out toothpicks to make it look as though they have had a good, filling meal. North Korea has a tremendous yearning for respect from the United States. They want to be treated as equals and on that basis to have normal diplomatic trade, aid, and investment relations with the Western world. They want the United States to do what it did for Vietnam in July 1993—basically to tell American directors on the boards of the World Bank, the Asian Development Bank, and other international financial institutions that the United States no longer objects to the extension of credit to North Korea so that North Korea can begin the process of restoring its credit.

The significance of asking for a light-water reactor, on one hand, is quite small. It takes six to ten years to build, while North Korea abandons construction on reactors currently under way and freezes its nuclear program. The real significance of the light-water reactor request is that it is a prestige project and requires sustained years of commitment from the United States. Thus to the North Koreans, the reactor is a sign of long-term commitment from the United States and its allies to be engaged with North Korea. This commitment by the United States is clearly North Korea's strategy.

What worries the North Koreans is a decline in importance of the nuclear issue—that somehow the United States might discover that the reactor program was really not worth the fuss. They worry that the United States will either walk away and forget the nuclear issue or will become preoccupied with Bosnia or Haiti again and ignore North Korea, letting them "stew in their own juices" until they collapse. They are afraid that the unstated, de facto American and South Korean policy toward North Korea is one of regime collapse and absorption by the South.

They are also afraid of the United States having a policy of ever-escalating preconditions. A U.S. negotiator with the North was asked, "Isn't it true that the United States will not have a third round of dialogue unless North Korea meets this, this, and this condition?" He responded, "Yes, it is true because there is no basis for the United States to trust North Korea. Moreover, the United States cannot permit a dialogue with the North Koreans while reprocessing continues behind its back in the meantime." While this position is understandable, making the continuation of dialogue dependent on North Korea's fulfillment of certain preconditions is problematic because it makes progress with North Korea nearly impossible. North Korea fears that once it complies (for instance, on the nuclear issue), a succession of demands will follow on other issues—for example, missile sales to the Middle East, human rights, past support for state terrorism, and so forth. As a result, North Korea feels that whatever concessions it makes, the United States must also make concessions, simultaneously and without preconditions. North Korea wants to negotiate and bargain as an equal. It is not asking that the United States meet preconditions first. It is not asking that the United States withdraw its troops from South Korea, which had been a long-standing request. In fact, North Koreans privately say they want U.S. troops to stay for a while to help maintain stability in Northeast Asia.

Again, the North Koreans have a tremendous sense of pride. They have long-standing historical grievances. Americans have a poor understanding of that fact. Likewise, the North Koreans need to understand that Americans also have historical grievances. These grievances need to be overcome with a policy of boldness and strength, and ultimately with an extended hand. As President Reagan said, "Trust but verify." The United States should keep its forces in South Korea strong but not bolster them in a way that would cause North Korea to jump to conclusions.

The United States should try to solve these issues and reconcile with North Korea while Kim Il Sung is alive. No one knows what will happen when he dies. The son is now revered on a level with his father, but whether he will have the same ability to lead, govern, and command as his father does remains to be seen. It would have been much easier to make a deal with Kim Il Sung than with his successor. When President Nixon went to China, he dealt with Mao, which allowed the entire Chinese view of the United States to change because Mao was the one to initiate that policy. Similarly, if the United States can engage Kim Il Sung and help the North Koreans embark on their own version of Chinese-style reforms (which is what the Chinese have been encouraging them to do for so long), Americans will have seized the right opportunity. That opportunity is lost once Kim Il Sung dies because instability may occur as a result in North Korea. One faction may support improving relations with the United States while another faction may not. This controversy could lead to civil war.

The United States is at a very critical moment in its relations with North Korea. The efforts of the Clinton administration and President Carter deserve a great deal of support. I hope for a great turnaround that will lead to peace in Korea and set in motion the process of reunification, perhaps by the end of the decade.

QUESTION: How was President Carter's visit initiated? Did he invite himself, or did the North Korean government invite him?

MR. BARRY: President Carter had a long-standing invitation from President Kim Il Sung dating from early 1991. It was given to him when a North Korean foreign ministry official visited the Carter Center in spring 1991. President Bush and Secretary Baker discouraged Carter from going during the Bush years.

The next attempt that President Carter made to visit North Korea was in February 1993. He spoke with Secretary of State Warren Christopher, but Christopher felt that it would not be advisable to send a former U.S. president so early in a new administration. Secretary Christopher advised Carter not to make the trip at the time. A few weeks later, North Korea withdrew from the Non-Proliferation Treaty, which created a much more serious situation.

The 1994 trip was initiated by President Carter. He contacted the North Korean office in New York to ensure that his invitation was still standing, which it was. Then he contacted Vice President Gore, who obtained President Clinton's permission.

QUESTION: What can justifiably be done if a nation, even North Korea, decides to withdraw from a treaty legally? Why doesn't North Korea have the right to become a nuclear power with a nuclear weapons capability?

MR. BARRY: The NPT provides for a nation's withdrawal if it believes its "supreme interests" are threatened. That was the North's stated reason for withdrawal. Some people would agree that both Koreas should have nuclear weapons, thus creating a peninsular balance of nuclear power. Alternatively, others argue for a nuclear-free zone in Northeast Asia. Actually, the 1991 inter-Korean denuclearization agreement calls for a reprocessing-free peninsula.

North Korea does not have high respect for the international system. Its problem is that it has been treated, in many ways rightly so, as a pariah nation. North Korea's dilemma is that it wants to change but without reforming its political system. North Koreans want economic reform, but keeping their political system is more important to them. The undertaking of Chinese-style economic reforms in North Korea at whatever pace and extent, however, will have a positive effect on the political system in the long run.

The harshness of North Korea's system is attributable to nationalism and tradition as well as communism. The North Koreans have now opened tombs of past kings to the public, something they never would have done in the past. They claim to have found the remains of Korea's mythical founder, Tangun. They are recognizing the fact that Korea has a glorious heritage, which is a positive development.

The one thing that is not negotiable is the status of Kim Il Sung and his son, yet their status does not have to remain frozen as Communist dictators. The goal of both Koreas is a unified nation. An agreeable way to achieve reunification might emerge over the next few years in which the Kims would play a pivotal role. It could come sooner rather than later. A fully unified state may not result, but a loose confederation of two states might form instead.

COMMENT: I think what North Korea and Kim Il Sung want is recognition from the United States. Whether or not they have nuclear weapons is not the important point here. This demand or wish is well justified because for a long time recognition has been one-sided. There has been no cross-recognition. All great powers surrounding North Korea recognize South Korea since the collapse of the Soviet Union. Half-recognition happened, meaning China and the Soviet Union recognized South Korea, but the United States and Japan did not recognize North Korea. Kim Il Sung is pretty frustrated. His demands are quite fair. Japan and the United States should recognize North Korea. Nuclear weapons are bargaining cards to draw American and international attention. North Korea does not intend to bomb South Korea or sell nuclear weapons to Iraq or Libya.

MR. BARRY: Many scholars are asking what happened to cross-recognition, which was first recommended by Secretary of State Henry Kissinger in the mid-1970s. By August 1992, the Communist side—Russia and China—recognized South Korea. Although Japan was on the way to recognizing North Korea, the nuclear issue stalled that process at the request of the United States. This situation is certainly a grievance of North Korea. It feels surrounded. Its perception is that its former allies now have a clear preference for South Korea.

At the most basic level, the North Koreans are looking for respect, dignity, and legitimacy. A recent request by Kim Il Sung to Cambodia's King Sihanouk is very telling. The king was asked by Kim Il Sung, "Since you speak to them, could you kindly convey to the Americans the following: 'This is like a strip search. You want us to take off our shirt, then our pants and socks. First you want to see this, and once you see this, you want to see that. We simply cannot do this. We have secrets.'" The North Korean perception is one of constant demands with nothing offered in exchange. Kim Il Sung told King Sihanouk that if this trend continues, a war may result. This kind of admission by Kim Il Sung is very significant.

QUESTION: It is my understanding that the existing nuclear facilities are not designed to produce power because they are not tied into the power network. Do you have any information on that aspect? Is power being generated?

MR. BARRY: There have been mixed signs on whether the North's 5 megawatt reactor was to be connected to a power grid. If it currently is not, the DPRK can claim it eventually will be. They assert that their entire nuclear program is for power generation. South Korea generates 70 or 80 percent of its electricity through large nuclear reactors—reactors vastly more powerful than what North Korea is now constructing. So whether or not North Korea's reactors will be tied to a power grid, it does have a dire need for power.

COMMENT: Your presentation is a good illustration of the fact that most real life situations in the world are very complicated. Too often when a crisis attracts public attention, the situation is excessively simplified. You have helped us step back and understand the entire situation. North Korea, South Korea, and the countries surrounding them will have to live with what happens, and they would much rather live with peace than war.

NARRATOR: This presentation has been enlightening, and we are grateful to Mr. Barry for helping us understand this complex situation.

EPILOGUE

When I finished this Miller Center Forum on 7 July 1994, I had no idea that while I had lunch with colleagues afterward, Kim Il Sung would die. He passed away of an apparent heart attack at 2:00 a.m. on 8 July, Pyongyang time (1:00 p.m., 7 July, Eastern time), although it was not formally announced until two days later. Kim Il Sung had ruled North Korea as premier or president since 1948, the longest-serving head of state in the world. What was not well known was that Kim had been seriously ill for some time, and that situation perhaps explains why the North hastened to defuel its 5 megawatt reactor. His son, Kim Jong Il, knew that his father would not live much longer and thus created the nuclear crisis of May-June 1994 to force a resolution of the nuclear issue while his father was still alive. As it turned out, his father died three weeks after meeting Jimmy Carter, leaving as his legacy the agreement through Carter to freeze the DPRK nuclear program in exchange for U.S. provision of light-water reactors. Unfortunately, Kim's other offer of a summit meeting with ROK President Kim Young Sam— originally scheduled for 25 July—was canceled after his death.

South Korea's reaction to Kim Il Sung's death was counterproductive, and it lost an irreplaceable opportunity to improve relations with the North. The ROK placed its military on high alert, refused to offer even *pro forma* condolences (other than being sorry to see the summit canceled). Moreover, with the help of Russian-supplied documents, it condemned Kim Il Sung for starting the Korean War. The South invoked its draconian National Security Law upon any citizen attempting to offer condolences, or worse, attempting to attend the funeral. Even President Clinton, U.N. Secretary-General Boutrous-Ghali, President Carter, and Reverend Billy Graham offered condolences. South Korea's contempt for Kim Il Sung was taken as a personal offense by Kim Jong Il, the successor, who has since been saying that belated condolences and abrogation of the National Security Law are the primary conditions to recommence the North-South dialogue. In short, North-South relations went downhill after Kim's death when the South gave up the opportunity to herald a new era by abandoning its zero-sum competition with the North and thus taking the magnanimous position of embracing its neighbor. The likelihood is that unless the South modifies its posture, the North will wait out Kim Young Sam's term as president of South Korea and deal with his successor in 1998.

The third round of U.S.-DPRK dialogue had just begun in Geneva on 8 July when the news came that Kim Il Sung had died. The talks were postponed until mid-August, whereupon the two sides, following up on the Carter agreement, quickly arrived at an "Agreed Statement," in which the outlines of a potential package deal took shape. The key issues that remained to be resolved were the need for North Korea to agree to special inspections of its undeclared nuclear facilities as part of its return to the NPT, North Korean acceptance of a South Korean model light-water reactor, and the central role Seoul would have to play in funding the project. These issues were hammered out in the succeeding weeks—despite a great deal of hesitation from Seoul that strained U.S.-ROK relations—so that by 21 October 1994, the two sides could sign what they called an Agreed Framework.

The main elements of the Agreed Framework were that Pyongyang would continue its freeze on its nuclear program and ultimately dismantle it (something not even required by the NPT), and it would return to the NPT as a full member and accept full-scope safeguards (meaning special inspections as well) before delivery of any critical light-water reactor components. The United States agreed to organize an international consortium called the Korean Peninsula Energy Development Organization (KEDO) to finance and supply two 1,000 megawatt (electric) light-water reactors, and in the interim to provide 500,000 tons of heavy fuel oil per year (as compensation for the approximate total power that the North's nuclear program, when complete, would have generated). In addition, the North agreed to allow the plutonium-rich spent fuel rods from its 5 megawatt reactor to be stored and eventually shipped to a third country. The two sides agreed to improve their bilateral relationship, beginning with progressive removal of trade restrictions and the opening of liaison offices in each other's capital, eventually leading, after resolution of other major issues, to

153

normalized relations. Finally, the North acknowledged that it was prepared to engage in direct dialogue with the South.

The Agreed Framework is just that; it is not a treaty or an executive agreement. Yet, it is a historical document on whose basis the nuclear issue is being resolved and U.S.-DPRK relations can commence and develop. It is also an important victory for Kim Jong Il in his efforts to secure his power base amidst transition to his leadership. The Agreed Framework has been roundly criticized by many in Congress, but much of that criticism has been the result of partisan politics, especially since the Republicans captured a congressional majority in November 1994. However, Congress wisely has avoided interfering with its implementation to date, aware that the agreement cannot be renegotiated and not wanting responsibility for heightened tensions in Korea. One year after its signing, the Agreed Framework appears to be a solid diplomatic achievement. The issue of ROK supply of its reactor type was resolved in June 1995, and a supply contract between KEDO and the DPRK is probable by year's end. U.S. and DPRK liaison offices in Pyongyang and Washington will likely open by spring 1996.

North-South relations have moved ahead far too little. One problem for the South is that Kim Jong Il has yet to assume either of his father's posts as party general secretary or president and remains simply commander in chief. Thus, Kim Young Sam is deprived of being able to hold a summit meeting. Kim Jong Il appears to be reluctant to assume the vacant posts, partly to appear as a humble and filial son to the North Korean populace and partly due to likely strategic issues still being sorted out within the elite, especially with the military. In summer 1995, the two Koreas did, however, hold a series of "rice talks" on the provision of rice when the economically desperate North admitted that "bad weather" had yielded a poor harvest. The South (along with Japan) decided to supply several hundred thousand tons of rice to the North. These talks have yet to expand to include political issues other than rice—if they continue at all. The North also suffered enormous flood damage in late summer and appealed for international disaster relief, something unprecedented in DPRK history. The United States decided to contribute a modest sum as disaster aid to North Korea. The South, aware that the winter of 1995-96 will be exceedingly difficult for the North, may withhold any upcoming offers or assistance and wait to see if the North will be reduced to a more willing bargaining position.

The Agreed Framework will remain the baseline of U.S.-DPRK relations for years to come. Thus far, it has withstood several tests with the North and undoubtedly will face future tests. Discontent in the United States over the framework is not likely to disappear quickly, as some critics contend the United States is delaying the collapse of a regime it does not like or that it has opened the door to other pariah states to expect deals with the United States. The real source of disapproval, however, is not so much in the specifics of the Agreed Framework but in the conviction of some that *any* American deal with North Korea is a bad deal. Thus, any U.S. agreement with the North was bound to be unpopular in some quarters, but it is important to see this package deal as a contribution toward peace and stability in Northeast Asia and as a first step toward the peaceful reunification of Korea. In the long run, it will be regarded as a brilliant stroke of negotiation by the Clinton administration.

CHAPTER NINE

North Korea and Nuclear Weapons

HAKJOON KIM

This chapter will try to analyze the present situation on the Korean Peninsula with emphasis upon the North Korean nuclear development issue and will try to set forth some policy implications for the two Koreas.

There is another element that disturbs the harmony of our view of the Asia-Pacific region. That is the proliferation of nuclear weapons in the region. Not to be overlooked either is the spread of chemical weapons and weapons of mass destruction. The fact that the majority of nations that possess chemical weapons are located in the Asia-Pacific region is something else that is amazing. Hee-Kwon Park mentions Burma, China, North Korea, Taiwan, and Vietnam as "probable" chemical weapons states, and Indonesia, Laos, South Korea, and Thailand as "possible" chemical weapons states. It is encouraging, however, that all regional countries with a chemical weapons capability except North Korea signed the chemical weapons convention in Paris on 13-15 January 1993.[1]

In relation to this, there is also another point that merits serious discussion: the development of nuclear weapons by North Korea. Ominous public pronouncements about North Korean nuclear development grew by leaps and bounds in 1993. In February, United States CIA Director R. James Woolsey told the Senate Committee on Governmental Affairs that there was "a real possibility" that North Korea had enough plutonium for a nuclear weapon. On 30 November, Woolsey said on CNN's "Larry King Live" that North Korea could have enough plutonium for one or perhaps two bombs. There is no evidence that North Korea already

157

has or is close to having a bomb.[2] It is now widely known, however, that at the very least, North Korea has amassed enough plutonium to manufacture one or two nuclear warheads. It has also been successful in testing the missile that would launch the nuclear warhead. With a range of 1,000 kilometers, all of South Korea and Western Japan is within the missile's range.[3]

North Korea's potential to become a nuclear nation has received wide criticism from the world community, including the United Nations. In mid-February 1993, the International Atomic Energy Agency (IAEA) called on North Korea to allow a "special inspection" of the North Korean nuclear facilities. North Korea rejected the demand. The IAEA then gave North Korea until 31 March 1993 to comply. The North reacted to the deadline by announcing on 12 March its decision to withdraw from the Non-Proliferation Treaty (NPT). The United States had two negotiations with North Korea in June 1993 in New York and in July in Geneva. The talks produced two joint statements. North Korea stated that it would suspend its withdrawal from the NPT as long as it considered it necessary. The United States gave North Korea assurances against the threat and use of force, including nuclear weapons. North Korea maintained the substance of its intended withdrawal from the NPT, however, by continuing until recently to reject the demand for a special inspection.[4]

How is it, then, that North Korea has not flinched from its position? Perhaps the answer to the question can be found in its domestic and foreign policy situation.

North Korea is mired in extreme difficulty in the economic realm. Its economy is continuing its downward slide for the fourth consecutive year since 1990. According to an authority on North Korea's economy—an economy chronically marred by the distorted allocation of resources caused by the need to meet political requirements and address the low worker morale both in agriculture and industry that is unique to a Communist command economy—North Korea's failed economy may have already lost its power of restitution and may be unable to bring itself back on its own feet. North Korea's snow-balling foreign debt is perhaps a testimony to the fact that a functioning national economy has indeed ceased to exist in North Korea. Remaining economic activities managed by the state are virtually confined to those directly associated with the upkeep of the Kim Il Sung regime.[5] As a result, North Korea's GNP is now less than a tenth the size of South Korea's GNP. There is insufficient oil to meet national needs following the Russian supply cutoff in 1991. Some observers estimate that industrial production is down by as much as 40 percent. Grain production has been declining, and North Korea has to import food grains. Food shortages have been reported, and the population has been urged to make do with just two meals a day.[6] Observers, viewing this situation, have even come to the point where they offer the theory of an "early collapse of the North Korean regime." One British North Korea watcher predicted that the North Korean regime would fall by 1997.[7]

Externally, North Korea has become extremely isolated. The former Soviet Union, a traditional ally and economic supporter, has fallen. Its heir, Russia, has drawn much closer to South Korea and in fact has abandoned almost all ties to the North. Ties with countries in Eastern Europe have cooled. Only China is giving the appearance of not forgetting old ties and is helping out, but China is also continuing to turn more in the direction of South Korea. On the other hand, the U.S. alliance with South Korea remains firm, and the Japanese relations with South Korea are fairly good.

Given its siege mentality, North Korea's ruling elites believe that its very survival is tied to the development of nuclear weapons. This is the bait it is using in its attempt to negotiate with the United States. The North wants to be granted diplomatic recognition and economic cooperation and be assured that the Kim Il Sung/Kim Jong Il dynasty can be continued. As for the assurance of the continuation of the Kim dynasty, North Korea asked for (1) permanent cancellation of the U.S.-South Korea "Team Spirit" exercise; (2) an American commitment to signing a mutual nonaggression agreement with North Korea; and (3) a so-called negative security guarantee for North Korea, meaning an American promise not to use nuclear weapons against the North. Then, says North Korea, it will relieve the West's suspicions regarding the development of nuclear weapons.[8]

If the United States were to establish diplomatic relations with North Korea, there is a strong likelihood that Japan would follow suit. Since Russia and China have already established their respective diplomatic relations with South Korea, the American and Japanese diplomatic decisions would mean the final realization of the cross-recognition of the two Koreas by the four major powers (the United States, Japan, China, and Russia). Then North Korea may enter into serious negotiations with South Korea for peaceful settlement. This will be the start of a new movement to change the current Korean armistice agreement of 1953 into a real peace agreement from which the two Koreas may move toward peaceful unification.

For a time, however, the North—in an effort to increase its own legitimacy and to downgrade the South Korean governmental authority—insisted on a high-level conference with the United States that excluded South Korea. The possibilities are great that they will not show sincerity toward the resumption of dialogue with the South.

Moreover, North Korea has given expression to one critically important possibility. In the words of Andrew Mack, "Pyongyang may see nuclear weapons, not as a 'nuclear card' to be bargained away, but as a vital strategic asset that must be maintained at almost any cost."[9] The reasons are obvious enough. Again, to borrow Mack's analysis:

Nuclear weapons would provide a countervailing deterrent against U.S. nuclear threats. These threats still exist in the form of the "nuclear umbrella" being another way of saying that under certain circumstances, the U.S. would use nuclear weapons against North Korea;

- nuclear weapons will act as a deterrent against the threat to the North posed by the overwhelming conventional military superiority that the South will achieve at some time during this decade;

- nuclear weapons will compensate the North for the loss of its nuclear ally, Russia;

- and nuclear weapons will ensure that North Korea is taken seriously as a major player in the region, even though its economy may be in crisis.[10]

If the North is determined to continue with its nuclear weapons program, it poses the most serious security threat on the Korean Peninsula. Certainly it is the dominant security issue on the Korean Peninsula. In my judgment, the North will not relinquish its nuclear option voluntarily. I contend that the security future of the Korean Peninsula appears pessimistic. Under such circumstances, South Korea must seriously and firmly go through a process to prepare to deal with North Korea. The South must maintain a stronger military alliance with the United States through the 1990s.

In the middle term—for example, up until the year 2000—without fail the North must undergo fundamental change. In the meantime, we know that Kim Il Sung will die. We can also forecast that as a result, this crisis will cause rapid reform. On the one hand, as Northeast Asia currently progresses with a "beyond barriers" economic cooperation stance, trade will also accelerate within the next few years. The huge wind that will blow as a result will also envelop the North.

Rinn-Sup Shinn has suggested that four outcome scenarios seem likely in North Korea in the 1990s: status quo, reform, hard-line, and collapse.[11] Nicholas Eberstadt has suggested three outcome scenarios: reform, "muddling through," or collapse.[12] As Eberstadt persuasively concludes, however, "forswearing reform, but doggedly attempting to muddle through, the regime will eventually face the prospect of breakdown or collapse."[13] Natalie Bazhanov also strongly contends that "sooner or later, the Communist regime in the North will collapse."[14] James Cotton's prediction is also pessimistic. He contends that "from the point of view of the dynamics of regime security, the North Korean leadership possesses few options." The only option may be an opening policy; however, it "will set in train the dissolution of the Kim Il Sung system."[15]

From that analysis we can see that the possibilities of North/South unification will be given a new decisive historical turning point. As many experts have pointed out, the possibilities are much greater that the unification of the Korean Peninsula will come about as an unexpected and unpredictable situation that breaks out in the North rather than the result of some well thought-out plan.

In that event, an initiative must, of course, come from South Korea. To make that possible, the South must make extensive efforts to prepare politically, economically, and diplomatically. In this context, the basic thesis of Thucydides's *History of the Peloponnesian War* may also be applicable to the two Koreas. The South should establish the virtuous cycle of "the growth-democracy-peace triangle." Only the forces of "the growth-democracy-peace triangle" have tended to work jointly to promote a more peaceful and stable regional order. If the South cannot do this, then unfortunately, the danger of interference from good-intentioned foreign powers, as well as those not so well intended, is great.

ENDNOTES

1. Hee-Kwon Park, "Multilateral Security Cooperation," *The Pacific Review*, vol. 6, no. 3 (1993), 260. His sources are Elisa D. Harris, "Chemical Weapons Proliferation: Current Capabilities and Prospects for Control," *New Threats, An Aspen Strategy Report*, 70-71.

2. David Albright, "North Korea and the 'Worst-Case' Scenario," *The Bulletin of the Atomic Scientists* (January-February 1994), 3.

3. Paul Bracken, "Nuclear Weapons and State Survival in North Korea," *Survival*, vol. 35, no. 3 (Autumn 1993), 145.

4. Larry A. Niksch, "North Korea's Nuclear Weapons Program." *CRS Issue Brief* (Washington, D.C.: Congressional Research Service, The Library of Congress, February 1994), 2-3.

5. Dong-Bok Lee, "North Korea: Trends and Prospects," a paper read at the Northeast Asia and Russia Conference held in Washington, D.C., on 17-18 March 1994 under the sponsorship of the Gaston Sigur Center for East Asian Studies of the George Washington University, 6.

6. Andrew Mack, "Introduction," in Andrew Mack (ed.), *Asian Flashpoint* (forthcoming, 1994), 12.

7. For example, see Aidan Foster-Carter, *Korea's Coming Reunification: Another East Asian Superpower?* (London: The Economist Intelligence Unit, 1992), 95.

8. For this view, see Andrew Mack, "The Nuclear Crisis on the Korean Peninsula," *Asian Survey*, vol. 33, no. 4 (April 1993), 359.

9. Mack, "Introduction," 9.

10. Ibid., 9-10.

11. Rinn-Sup Shinn, "North Korea: Policy Determinants, Alternative Outcomes, U.S. Policy Approaches," *CRS Report for Congress* (Washington, D.C.: Congressional Research Service, the Library of Congress, June 1993), 14-18.

12. Nicholas Eberstadt, "North Korea: Reform, Muddling Through, or Collapse?" *NBR Analysis*, vol. 4, no. 3 (September 1993), 12-16.

13. Ibid., 18.

14. Natalie Bazhanov, "Russia's Relations with North Korea," a paper read at the Northeast Asia and Russia Seminar held at Washington, D.C., on 17-18 March 1994, under the sponsorship of the Gaston Sigur Center for East Asian Studies, George Washington University, 18.

15. James Cotton, "North Korea's Nuclear Ambitions," *Adelphi Paper*, no. 275 (March 1993), 104-105.

V.

THE HISTORY
OF A CRISIS

CHAPTER TEN

North Korea's Dangerous Nuclear Deal, Process, and Prospect*

HYOUNG-CHAN CHOE

INTRODUCTION

The conference of the states party to the Non-Proliferation Treaty (NPT) convened in New York on 17 April 1995 and met for almost one month to make a decision on the fate of the treaty, which is going to expire on the last day of this year. At the conference, the group of Western countries, including the five nuclear powers, advocated indefinite extension of the treaty, whereas the nonaligned countries, including North Korea, opposed the proposal, arguing that the nuclear-weapon states had not adequately carried out their obligation of nuclear disarmament under the treaty. Thanks to intensive U.S. efforts to persuade countries whose positions were flexible and the nonaligned countries' failure to unite, however, the countries participating in the conference eventually decided in May 1995 that the treaty should continue in force indefinitely. North Korea did not participate in the final meeting in which the decision was made.

North Korean authorities have continued to argue that Pyongyang has neither the intention nor capability to develop nuclear weapons. If North Korea were such a peace-loving state, why could it not actively support the indefinite extension of the

---

*Hyoung-Chan Choe is assistant director of the North America Division II at the Ministry of Foreign Affairs in Seoul, South Korea.

NPT, which is to prevent vertical and horizontal nuclear proliferation?

North Korea's nuclear program, involving an indigenous 5MWe graphite-moderated reactor and a plutonium reprocessing plant, which North Korea calls the radio-chemical laboratory, caught the attention of surrounding countries from at least the early 1980s. Since then, a duel between North Korea and countries concerned about North Korea's ambition has begun.

NONCOMPLIANCE WITH THE NONPROLIFERATION REGIME

The steady, indigenous nuclear program of North Korea generated growing concern in the international community, in particular that of the United States, in terms of nuclear nonproliferation. When North Korea finally joined the NPT under the pressure of the former Soviet Union in 1985, the international community was reassured.[1] Soviet officials seem to have used two arguments. First, they warned that four light-water reactors promised by President Chernenko a year earlier would not be provided unless the North consented to become a member of the NPT. Second, they claimed that signing the treaty would help persuade the United States to withdraw its nuclear weapons from South Korea. Despite joining the NPT, North Korea did not give up its nuclear development program. Rather, North Korea vigorously expanded its activities at Yongbyon and embarked on strengthening its nuclear development program, which included a plutonium reprocessing plant. Furthermore, Pyongyang did not execute what the NPT required of signatories–the conclusion of a safeguards agreement with the IAEA within 18 months after signing the treaty. As it happened, Chernenko's successor, Mikhail Gorbachev, reneged on the reactor deal.[2] Delaying the requirement, Pyongyang instead set two preconditions for reaching the safeguards agreement: first, the withdrawal of all U.S. nuclear weapons from the South, and second, a "negative security assurance" (NSA) from the United States; that is, a guarantee that the United States would not use nuclear weapons against the North.[3] The occasion that would break the stalemate happened much sooner than expected. On 27 September 1991, President George Bush announced the decision to withdraw tactical nuclear weapons from Asia and Europe, which cleared the way for the North to sign the safeguards agreement. Immediately following this decision, a spokesman for the North Korean Foreign Ministry welcomed the decision and Kim Yong-Sun, secretary for the international affairs of the Central Committee of the Worker's Party of North Korea, stated that the North may accept international inspection of its nuclear facilities if the United States withdraws its nuclear weapons from South Korea.[4] Although only one of the two preconditions that North Korea had set was fulfilled, the second one was actually being dropped as a precondition for signing the safeguards.[5]

Dramatic improvements of relations between the two Koreas also played an important role in making the North change its mind. South Korean President Roh Tae Woo officially declared on 18 December 1991 that there were no nuclear weapons in South Korea. The North quickly welcomed the announcement, claiming that its "consistent and just demand has been fulfilled at last."[6] Furthermore, the two Korean governments signed two agreements in December 1991, one of which was for reconciliation, cooperation, and nonaggression between the two sides, and the other for denuclearization of the Korean Peninsula. Under these favorable circumstances, the South and the North received what they wanted from each other: On 7 January 1992, Seoul announced the decision to suspend the 1992 U.S.-South Korean joint military "Team Spirit" exercise, which Pyongyang had attacked as a nuclear war exercise against North Korea.[7] In return, Pyongyang announced that it would sign a full-scope safeguards agreement with the IAEA. Meanwhile, the U.S. government, for the first time, held talks with a North Korean high-ranking official in America to encourage the North to sign the safeguards agreement with the IAEA as soon as possible (details are mentioned later). After having been the signatory to the NPT for over six years, Pyongyang finally signed the safeguards agreement with the IAEA in January and ratified it in April 1992. Suspicion among Western countries over North Korea's nuclear development program was once again assuaged.

Pyongyang handed over to the IAEA its initial inventory report on nuclear material and provided design information on seven nuclear facilities in North Korea. The first IAEA inspection began on 25 May 1992. The IAEA had inspected the seven declared nuclear facilities of North Korea six times between May 1992 and February 1993. Parallel to the IAEA inspections, the South-North Joint Nuclear Control Commission, which was formed under the "Joint Declaration on Denuclearization of the Korean Peninsula," continued discussions about mutual nuclear inspections of each other's nuclear facilities. As the IAEA inspections went on, however, the optimistic view that a rational solution of the North Korean nuclear issue could be found began to erode. During the inspection by agency officials in January-February 1993, the inspectors of the U.N. watchdog discovered "significant inconsistencies" between North Korea's report and IAEA's experiment on the quantity of plutonium extracted from spent fuel. Consequently, on 9 February, IAEA Director-General Hans Blix asked North Korea to provide additional information to clear up inconsistencies about its past plutonium reprocessing activities and asked for a "special inspection," a request never before made of any state by the IAEA, of two undeclared nuclear sites.[8] A more expanded implementation of the IAEA's mandate and an appropriate use of information given to the agency—a U.S. spy satellite imagery showed the North Koreans building walls and sentry posts around the nuclear waste site—detected North Korea's undeclared sites suspected of illegal nuclear activities. Moreover, in December 1992, Russian security forces had stopped 36 senior weapons scientists from flying to Pyongyang, where they were suspected of taking part in North Korea's nuclear program for large salaries. Russia's Foreign Intelligence Service—successor to the KGB—also confirmed that North Korea was continuing its nuclear development program and had reached the stage of being able to make a nuclear bomb.[9] North Korea, however, refused the IAEA's request for a special inspection. Meanwhile, the inter-Korean nuclear talks had made little progress and could not go on to further rounds.[10]

On 25 February, the IAEA Board of Governors backed the director-general's request in a resolution calling on North Korea to accept a special inspection of its two undeclared sites—where nuclear waste was thought to be dumped after reprocessing—in an effort to determine whether Pyongyang, despite its insistent denials, had produced enough plutonium to make a nuclear bomb. The deadline for complying with the request was 25 March. A war of nerves began. Since North Korea did not show any compliance with the IAEA request, South Korea and the United States announced the decision to launch the Team Spirit joint military exercise on 7 March, which had been suspended in the previous year. In response, the supreme commander of North Korea's People's Army, Kim Jong Il, ordered a state of "semi-war," which had been ordered only two times during the past four decades since the Korean War. Then on 12 March, Pyongyang announced the decision to withdraw from the NPT and denied IAEA access to the suspected nuclear waste sites, claiming that those were military bases and not related to the nuclear program.

INTERNATIONAL EFFORTS TO CURB NORTH KOREA

The First Phase (March 1993-May 1993):
Standoff between North Korea and the International Community

The unexpected response by North Korea alarmed the international community, in particular, Seoul and Washington. For its part, South Korea would have a more hostile and powerful Communist regime equipped with nuclear weapons next to it on the Korean Peninsula. For the United States, failure to inhibit North Korea from developing nuclear arms would harm more than its national interests. First, regional nonproliferation would be undermined by the North Korean program because the development of nuclear weapons by North Korea would directly intimidate the two major U.S. allies in the region—South Korea and Japan. Second, a withdrawal by North Korea from the NPT and develop-ment of a nuclear weapons capability by North Korea could seriously degrade efforts to control international proliferation through the IAEA. Finally, if North Korea acquires nuclear weapons, it threatens the balance in the current environment of the region. Its internal instability could provoke an attack on South

Korea in an act of desperation. A war on the Korean Peninsula would severely harm the stability of the region and hence the economic interests of the United States.[11] Once North Korea was out of the NPT, there would be no legal, systematic apparatus to check North Korea's nuclear development efforts.[12] Furthermore, it would become legally and systematically difficult to block North Korea from making as many as 50 nuclear weapons annually by the year 2000[13] and selling the nuclear material, technology, or a nuclear weapon itself to other nuclear aspirants such as Iran, Iraq, or Libya. In addition, a precedent of withdrawal from the NPT would endanger the very existence of the NPT itself.

Under these grave circumstances, Seoul and Washington at first agreed to resolve the North Korean nuclear issue through the United Nations and the IAEA, since these international organizations were the parties legally related to the matter. Having received no positive response from Pyongyang by the end of March, the IAEA referred North Korea's nuclear issue to the U.N. Security Council by the next day, thus passing the ball to the council. However, continuous official statements of the Communist regime that a solution to the nuclear issue on the Korean Peninsula could be found through direct dialogue between the United States and North Korea, persuaded U.S. decisionmakers to consider high-level talks with North Korea.[14] As grounds for its claim, North Korea argued that it had neither power nor will to develop nuclear weapons and that the nuclear issue in the Korean Peninsula was initiated not by the so-called nuclear weapons program of North Korea, but by the tactical nuclear weapons of the United States in South Korea and developed by the remaining threat of U.S. nuclear attack against North Korea. Responding to the North's bid to hold talks with the United States, the State Department announced that the United States would not rule out a high-level meeting with North Korea to solve the nuclear problems. The South Korean foreign minister declared that Seoul would not oppose the United States holding high-level talks with the North. In this context, the U.N. Security Council, which was supposed to take measures, including sanctions against the Stalinist regime, passed a low-keyed resolution in May, requesting that North Korea reconsider its decision to withdraw from the NPT and comply with its nuclear safeguards agreement with the IAEA. More important, the resolution provided the United States with the ground to negotiate with North Korea by stating that all member states are urged to encourage North Korea to respond positively to the resolution.[15]

The Second Phase (June 1993–July 1993):
Talks between Washington and Pyongyang

As seen above, North Korea had taken the advantage of the improbable U.S. nuclear threat as a pretext for negotiation with the United States. North Korea's desire to enter into discussions with the United States, however, had been expressed earlier. In March 1974, North Korea proposed to enter into talks with the United States to the exclusion of South Korea and asserted that through the talks, the current armistice agreement in effect on the Korean Peninsula be converted into a peace treaty. The United States turned down the proposal on the grounds that Korean problems must be resolved directly between South and North Korea.[16]

It took more than a dozen years for the United States to respond favorably to the idea of talks with North Korea. The South Korean government announced on 7 July 1993 that it intended to establish diplomatic relations with the Soviet Union and the PRC, both allies of North Korea. In return, South Korea would not oppose North Korea's moves to establish relations with Japan and the United States. The United States took advantage of South Korea's new policy and entered discussions with North Korea through their counselors in Beijing; however, the discussions were understood to be informal and not formal government-to-government-level discussions.[17]

The first response to high-level talks with North Korea occurred in January 1992. To encourage North Korea to sign the nuclear safeguards accord with the IAEA, U.S. Undersecretary of State Arnold Kanter held discussions in New York with Kim Yong-Sun, who was in charge of international affairs for the North Korean Worker's Party. The discussions were productive in that they contributed to accomplishing the objectives of both countries: opening high-level talks with the United States for the North

Korean side and signing of the safeguards agreement of Pyongyang with the IAEA for the U.S. side.[18]

Although the U.S. government did not want to negotiate with North Korea at first, there was no good reason for the United States, which already had more high-level contact with North Korea, to intentionally look down on North Korea's explicit and implicit demand for high-level discussions when such a serious issue as nuclear proliferation was at stake. North Korea's withdrawal from the NPT would have been a heavy burden for the United States if left unresolved. Moreover, the new Clinton administration, which had only been in office for a few months, was anxious to score some diplomatic points by successfully negotiating with North Korea on behalf of the world community.

At last, a North Korean delegation led by First Vice Foreign Minister Kang Sok-Ju and a U.S. delegation led by Assistant Secretary of State for Political and Military Affairs Robert Gallucci opened the first round of high-level talks in New York in June 1993. As a result of the four sessions of negotiation, Pyongyang agreed to suspend its decision to withdraw from the NPT on 11 June, just one day before the withdrawal of the NPT was to take effect. In return, the United States gave North Korea assurances against the threat and use of force, including that of nuclear weapons.[19] In the statement, both sides also expressed their support for the impartial application of full-scope IAEA safeguards, although the North did not agree to accept special inspections at the two suspected nuclear waste storage sites. The joint statement also expressed support for the North-South declaration on the denuclearization of the Korean Peninsula.[20] On that which the two sides agreed, however, they seemed not to agree on which points should be stressed. First, the North tried to classify the U.S.-North Korean high-level talks as a "political" negotiation. This is in accordance with its consistent propaganda that the nuclear issue of the Korean Peninsula should be resolved by political negotiation between Pyongyang and Washington. Second, Pyongyang made an effort to pay little attention to the issue of rejoining the NPT. Third, Pyongyang appeared to have no intention of allowing the special inspection. Finally, the North was not really interested in talks with the South. The reason that Pyongyang stressed the "impartiality" of the IAEA seems to reveal the North's desire that the IAEA rescind its unfair–from the perspective of Pyongyang–request for a special inspection.

At a press conference, remarks of Kang Sok-Ju on the release of the joint statement demonstrate well these points. He evaluated the meeting as "political," dealing with policies, and stressed that the two sides agreed not to pose a nuclear threat to each other, to respect each other's systems and sovereignty, and not to interfere in each other's internal affairs. Claiming the talks as successful, he also argued that the temporary suspension of North Korea's withdrawal from the NPT was the decision of North Korea itself. With respect to the issue of IAEA inspections, he gave no indication that Pyongyang would let inspectors look into the two suspected nuclear sites. Instead, Kang demanded the "impartiality" of the IAEA. He did not mention at all the South-North Joint Declaration on the Denuclearization of the Korean Peninsula, which the North agreed to support in the statement.[21]

On the other hand, Gallucci appeared less pleased that the two sides had not reached a complete accord. However, American diplomats said that they intended to seek a new round of talks to persuade North Korea to complete its change of course while expressing relief that the deadline would pass without the standoff turning into a rupture.[22] American diplomats appear to have not noticed North Korea's intention not to accept a special inspection by the IAEA or its intention not to develop the inter-Korean dialogue. Pyongyang's sole concerns lay in further negotiation with Washington.

On 26 June, North Korea's premier withdrew his own proposal for an exchange of special presidential envoys between Seoul and Pyongyang. On 1 July, an IAEA spokesman stated that North Korea had rejected an IAEA proposal to discuss the resumption of inspections of its nuclear facilities before the second set of high-level talks with the United States. On the contrary, Pyongyang showed a reconciliatory gesture toward Washington by handing over the remains of 17 U.S. servicemen listed as killed in action during the Korean War to the United States at the truce village of Panmunjom.

One month after the first round of high-level talks, the delegates of the two governments, headed by the same chiefs as those of the first-round talks, held the second round of high-level talks in Geneva. At the first session, the United States called on North Korea to have talks with the IAEA on ad hoc IAEA inspections and emphasized the importance of the South-North dialogue. In response, North Korea disputed the impartiality of the IAEA and attributed the failure of the exchange of special envoys between Seoul and Pyongyang to South Korea. The North demanded again that the United States guarantee its non-use of nuclear weapons against North Korea and suspend the Team Spirit joint military exercises. At the second session, however, North Korea abruptly brought on the agenda the issue of converting a current graphite reactor to a light-water reactor,[23] saying that if the United States assists in the replacement of the reactors, it would discuss with the IAEA the inspection issue and resume the South-North dialogue.[24] Not prepared for North Korea's unexpected suggestion, the U.S. delegates needed time to analyze the implications of the suggestion. At the third session, the United States agreed to accept the offer in a bid to keep the North within the nonproliferation regime such as the NPT, the IAEA, and the South-North Joint Declaration on the Denuclearization of the Korean Peninsula. In a joint statement after the talks, the two sides agreed that North Korea was prepared to begin consultations with the IAEA on outstanding safeguards and with South Korea on bilateral issues, including the nuclear issue, as soon as possible. The joint statement also reaffirmed U.S. assurances against the threat and use of force, including that of nuclear weapons, and announced U.S. agreement to support the conversion of North Korea's gas graphite reactors into light-water reactors.[25]

Gallucci, the head of the U.S. delegation, stated that the talks had made "small but significant" progress.[26] Presenting the U.S. view of the agreement, he stressed that North Korea agreed to begin consultation with the IAEA on outstanding safeguards issues, including the IAEA's requests for additional information and visits to additional sites. Although the United States failed to obtain North Korea's agreement to accept a special inspection, it hoped Pyongyang would allow the inspection through further consultations with the IAEA. In addition, he underlined that Pyongyang agreed to resume discussions with Seoul on the nuclear issue. Washington hoped that an effective bilateral inspection regime made through negotiations by the two Koreas would complement the international efforts to resolve the nuclear issue. Finally, he said that if the North would unambiguously comply with nonproliferation obligations, the United States would support the conversion of graphite reactors into light-water reactors, which are less suitable for nuclear weapons material production.[27]

Unlike Gallucci's understatement, Kang Sok-Ju claimed that the talks were "forward-looking and productive," arguing that replacing the reactors with light-water ones was an issue that made North Korea's nuclear transparency clear and suggested that the North had no intent of developing nuclear weapons. Concerning the talks with the IAEA and South Korea, he argued again that talks with the IAEA would begin based on the impartiality of the agency and that inter-Koreans relations could be improved by the realization of a summit meeting to whose end the exchange of special envoys was important.

The Third Phase (August 1993-June 1994):
North Korea's Denunciation and Modification Tactics

Not surprisingly, North Korea did not implement its agreement to consult with the IAEA on outstanding safeguards, such as the inspection of suspected nuclear sites and to resume talks with South Korea. Although the North accepted IAEA's ad hoc inspection team in August, the North blocked the inspectors' full access to key parts of the two problematic facilities capable of producing plutonium. No further progress was made between Pyongyang and the international nuclear proliferation watchdog on the issue of full implementation of the safeguards accord. Therefore, the IAEA took action to adopt a resolution on 1 October 1993 in its General Session to urge North Korea to prove it was not making nuclear weapons by submitting to the IAEA inspections.

Meanwhile, the two Koreas failed to discuss the implementation of the Joint Declaration, under which they were supposed to form a mutual inspection regime. Seoul, which had preferred to hold a meeting of the Joint Nuclear Control

Commission—the execution body of the Joint Declaration—agreed to hold working-level meetings for the exchange of presidential emissaries for the summit talks between the two Koreas, which Pyongyang preferred; Pyongyang, after just one perfunctory contact, rejected sending its delegates to the inter-Korean contacts thereafter.

Rejecting the offer of both the IAEA and Seoul vis-à-vis the nuclear issue, Pyongyang instead reiterated its consistent and desperate argument. On 5 October, one of the North Korean vice foreign ministers criticized the IAEA in a keynote speech given at the 48th U.N. General Assembly for having infringed on the sovereignty of North Korea by adopting an unrighteous resolution against it and stressed that the nuclear issue regarding the Korean Peninsula was a political issue to be solved only through bilateral negotiations with the United States. Worse yet, the North refused to accept even the ad hoc inspections of the IAEA, announcing on 12 October that it would no longer talk with the IAEA.[28] Under these circumstances, the United States carried out secret diplomatic contacts with North Korea in New York to break the deadlock over Pyongyang's refusal to allow IAEA inspections. However, the secret contacts failed to bring about resolutions concerning the nuclear issue.

Once again, as the IAEA and the United States had warned North Korea, the nuclear issue of North Korea was sent to the United Nations, and on 1 November 1993, the United Nations General Assembly adopted a resolution urging North Korea to allow IAEA inspectors into its nuclear facilities. Though the resolution of the U.N. General Assembly had no binding force against North Korea, North Korea might have felt international pressure, having seen the voting results in which only North Korea voted against the resolution while 140 nations voted for it.

While pressing Pyongyang in the international arena, the United States continued its effort to move out of the nuclear impasse through unofficial sessions with the North in New York. As the two sides were not narrowing their gaps in opinion concerning the nuclear issue, on 11 November Kang Sok-Ju, who led the Pyongyang delegation in the first and second rounds of talks with the United States, proposed to the United States the formula of a "package solution" for the nuclear issue, whereby the two sides would define what each side would do and carry out at the same time. In the statement he said that the major cause of the stalemate in generating a solution lay in the lack of trust between North Korea and the United States.[29] The next day, evaluating the offer as a signal of the North's positive change of position, a U.S. State Department spokesman said that the United States was prepared to discuss the deal as proposed by the North to resolve the nuclear issue. At this moment, the U.S. government set aside for the moment any discussion of special inspections at the suspected nuclear sites.[30] Moreover, Washington gave its highest-level response when President Clinton announced a "comprehensive approach" to the North Korean nuclear issue.[31]

When it comes to renunciation and modification of agreements, North Korea has been very skillful throughout the entire process of negotiation with the United States. Its tactic has been to rest on brinkmanship, placing its counterparts at bay, making them eager to get out of the stalemate as soon as possible, thereby getting modification of original agreements. This time the North was able to have the United States concede one of the two preconditions for holding a third round of talks with Washington.

It is precisely this soft approach that made the South Korean government uncomfortable. While Seoul had been unhappy about the North's attempt to exclude it from the nuclear debate, it wanted to avoid a situation in which it was relegated to a mere observer of the U.S.-North Korean talks. In a bid not to be excluded from the talks between Washington and Pyongyang, Seoul insisted that in place of a "comprehensive" approach, a "thorough and broad" negotiating approach was needed and that one precondition for the third round of U.S.-North Korean high-level talks would have to include "significant" progress in South-North talks on the nuclear problem.[32] Although Seoul and Washington cooperated in dealing with the North Korean nuclear issue to a large extent, they often took different approaches toward the North throughout the entire process of the nuclear deal with Pyongyang. This was the first split between Seoul and Washington over how to handle North Korea. On the basis of the tacit agreement, U.S. and North Korean diplomats met several times in New York over the IAEA regular inspections, and on 29 December, they reached a compromise: In exchange for the IAEA inspections of North Korea's declared nuclear sites, the United States would cancel its 1994 Team Spirit military exercises with South Korea.

In compliance with the promise, the negotiation between North Korea and the IAEA began in early January 1994. It stumbled, however, over the barrier set up by the North. Pyongyang argued that it had not agreed to ad hoc or routine inspection pursuant to the obligation under the NPT[33] and that the inspection of the IAEA should be restricted to only five reported nuclear facilities, except for the 5-megawatt reactor and the radio-chemical laboratory, which was involved with plutonium extraction.[34] In response, the IAEA stressed full-scope inspection for the seven nuclear facilities of North Korea, saying that it was up to the agency to decide what inspections it needed.[35] The decision between the two sides moved into a blind alley. Tensions surrounding the nuclear issue mounted high.

On 31 January 1994, Pyongyang warned that it would not be bound by the promise to suspend its decision to withdraw from the NPT.[36] It provided good ground for American hawks to press for a sterner approach by the Clinton administration to Pyongyang. On 1 February, the U.S. Senate passed a resolution calling on President Clinton to prepare to reintroduce tactical nuclear weapons to South Korea unless Pyongyang behaved. The renewed recalcitrance of the North led the U.S. government to seriously consider sanctions against it. On 4 February, the United States appealed to China, which would be a key factor for an efficient implementation of sanctions, to put pressure on North Korea to open its nuclear installations to the IAEA inspections. China had opposed the option, claiming that the nuclear issue should be solved through dialogue. The United States also warned that it would start pressing for U.N. Security Council sanctions against the North Korean government if it had not done so by 21 February. From that day, the IAEA Board of Governors was supposed to begin discussing North Korea's noncompliance with its safeguards agreement and refer to the U.N. Security Council.[37]

Washington had warned Pyongyang of the probability of sanctions whenever the latter broke its promises. This was the first real action taken by the United States to seriously take into consideration the sanctions option against the North in the U.N. Security Council meeting. In response, Pyongyang argued that it would consider any kind of sanction to be akin to a declaration of war. Meanwhile, Washington agreed to deploy Patriot missile batteries in South Korea to reassure the South.[38] While the tit for tat between Washington and Pyongyang continued, the sense of crisis was mounting in the press reports of America.[39]

Under this ever-growing tension, Seoul was convinced that hard-line measures against Pyongyang were likely to backfire. President Kim, fearing a rise in tension along the demilitarized zone, wanted to make absolutely sure that all possible measures had been explored and exhausted before the U.N. Security Council opted for sanctions.[40] This was the second case that revealed the difference of approach between Seoul and Washington toward North Korea. This course represented a considerable change in Seoul's position from November, when it openly complained that the United States was being too conciliatory with Pyongyang. Now, as the Clinton administration moved toward a harder line on North Korea, Seoul insisted that the doors should be kept wide open to talks even after the issue moved to the United Nations. South Korea did not want the United States and North Korea to get together without permission, but neither did it want war in the Korean Peninsula against its will. As the North's nuclear issue developed, it became clear that the United States and South Korea held different ideas about whether the special inspection of the IAEA or significant progress in South-North talks should be the preconditions for the third round of talks between Washington and Pyongyang, although neither Seoul nor Washington would acknowledge the difference in their policy toward Pyongyang. For its part, Pyongyang has opportunely taken advantage of the split in opinion between Seoul and Washington.

For all its heated threats, North Korea appears to have been afraid that the Security Council would impose sanctions against it. First, with both official and unofficial communication channels to Washington clogged, Pyongyang invited the Reverend Billy Graham, who continued to be friends with Kim Il Sung and had influence in American society, to deliver Kim Il Sung's personal message to

President Clinton. As the United States' firm position to impose sanctions against North Korea was not assuaged, despite Kim's gesture, the North felt it necessary to circumvent any talk of sanctions at the IAEA Board of Governors' meeting. Just six days before the meeting was held, North Korea finally agreed, in a letter delivered to the IAEA, to permit the IAEA inspection of its seven declared nuclear sites.[41]

In response to Pyongyang's move, the United States restarted informal talks with North Korea in New York. As an IAEA inspection team arrived in North Korea and as South and North Korea resumed talks on the exchange of special envoys who would address the nuclear issue, the United States announced on 3 March the suspension of the Team Spirit 1994 joint military exercise and agreed with the North to meet in Geneva on 21 March to begin a third round of negotiations.[42] At the same time, the U.S. undersecretary for international security affairs, Lynn Davis of the State Department, underlined that the United States would not hold the third round of talks until the inspections for the following reasons: to ensure that no nuclear material had been diverted since earlier inspections; to facilitate future verification of nondiversion; and to ensure that a "serious" discussion on the nuclear issue would occur between the South and North.[43] According to her statement, the United States seems to have not abandoned its hope that the South and North would develop a complementary mutual inspection regime under the principle of their joint denuclearization declaration through a continuous dialogue at least until the statement was issued.

After more than a year since the last regular inspections, an IAEA inspection team was allowed back to the seven nuclear sites at the Yongbyon nuclear complex. Nothing unusual was found at six of the sites, but at the seventh, the radio-chemical laboratory where plutonium could be extracted from nuclear fuel rods, the team was not permitted to take samples and smears from a glove box. Neither was it allowed to map gamma rays at waste gas disposal facilities, which were essential to reveal any recent handling of the North's plutonium stocks. North Korea, which had agreed to the sampling and mapping before the inspection team arrived, claimed that it would not allow the inspection because the

182

inspection was related with the problem of the earlier discrepancies between the North and the IAEA over the amount of extracted plutonium. Reporting that the truncated inspection prevented any meaningful conclusion about whether the North had diverted nuclear material for possible use in weapons, Hans Blix, director general of the IAEA, turned the matter over to the U.N. Security Council on 21 March.

Once again tensions surrounding the nuclear issue of North Korea rose high. At a working-level meeting between the South and North held at Panmunjom, a North Korean representative warned with prepared provocative words that "Seoul is not far from here. Should a war break out, Seoul will be a sea of fire." Toward the United States, the North also began expressing its irritation by proclaiming that the Korean Peninsula was on the brink of war and pointedly reminded the United States not to forget hundreds of thousands of deaths of American soldiers during the Korean War.[44] The U.S. government postponed the third round of high-level talks that was scheduled to be held with North Korea on 21 March, shipped Patriot missile batteries to South Korea, and began preparing for resuming the Team Spirit military exercises with South Korea. Moreover, in the U.N. Security Council, the United States was preparing a draft resolution warning North Korea of economic sanctions.

The Clinton administration's tough stance, however, had to be modified, facing China's strong opposition to sanctions against the North. Without China's participation in the sanctions, international sanctions could not harm North Korea. Beijing, the sole close friend of Pyongyang, had provided about three-quarters of North Korea's critical oil and food imports since the collapse of the Soviet Union and the democratization of Eastern European countries. China, however, had consistently been in opposition to pressing North Korea. It claimed that pressure such as economic sanctions might push the North's rickety economy to collapse. In this case, Beijing argued, if Pyongyang takes an extreme measure such as a military action against the South, it will have only limited power to control Pyongyang.[45] Therefore, the United States, realizing that economic sanctions against the North without China's help would not prove fruitful and failing to acquire the help from China, moderated its draft prepared for the U.N. Security Council. On 31 March, the U.N. Security Council issued a presidential statement, not a resolution more demanding in characteristics, calling on the North just to allow IAEA inspectors to finish their work at Yongbyon instead of threatening economic sanctions.

Once the United States and North Korea began to denounce each other, only the war of nerves continued and tensions surrounding the Korean Peninsula mounted higher and higher. Meanwhile, in an effort to break the impasse, pave the way for renewed international inspections in North Korea, and increase high-level dialogue between Washington and Pyongyang, Seoul made a major concession to North Korea: South Korean deputy prime minister and minister for unification announced that "we are no longer pushing for the exchange" of envoys, which the North had repeatedly refused.[46] By doing so, Seoul let Washington concentrate on the inspection issue alone. Seoul's sudden shift of position should be evaluated as a thoughtful diplomatic action because as the talks between the South and the North stagnated and finally reached an impasse, the United States came to feel it burdensome to maintain the South-North talks as a precondition for further talks with Pyongyang.[47] On the other hand, Pyongyang saw it as another victory over the nuclear issue through its hackneyed renunciation tactic.

Unfortunately, in spite of Seoul's positive gesture, Pyongyang did not change its course in a favorable way. On the contrary, it went in the opposite direction. Pyongyang, which blocked access of IAEA inspectors to the plutonium reprocessing plant, informed the IAEA that it intended to shut down the 5MWe nuclear reactor for refueling. It was a significant situation in that by analyzing the spent fuel, scientists could determine whether original fuel rods had been removed to produce plutonium and replaced with newer fuel.[48] The IAEA immediately told the North—as it had already told the North in February 1993—that it wished to select a number of fuel rods, segregate them from the others, and secure them for later examination during the refueling so that they would not be replaced by others.[49] Pyongyang turned down the suggestion, and to the international community's surprise, it began unloading fuel rods of the 5MWe reactor with no IAEA inspectors present.

184

Although it reluctantly accepted an IAEA inspection team on 17 May, it did not allow the inspectors to select rods and examine them, claiming again North Korea's unique status with respect to the NPT. Meanwhile, about 8,000 fuel rods from which enough plutonium for four or five nuclear weapons could be extracted had been discharged from the 5MWe reactor in two weeks.

At this stage, Hans Blix, director-general of the IAEA, reported to the Board of Governors that the limited opportunity that remained for the agency to select, segregate, and secure fuel rods from the North's 5MWe reactor for later measurements had been lost and that the agency's ability to ascertain whether nuclear material from the reactor had been diverted in the past had also been lost. The IAEA board adopted a resolution on 10 June, which stated that Pyongyang was widening its noncompliance with the safeguards agreement and that IAEA was suspending nonmedical IAEA assistance to the North. It furthermore urged the North's full cooperation for the implementation of safeguards.[50] In response, the North decided to withdraw from the IAEA as of 13 June. This action seemed to go beyond the realm of diplomatic debate.

President Clinton said, "North Korea's actions have made it virtually imperative that the Security Council consider sanctions." U.N. Ambassador Albright announced that she would immediately begin consulting with other members of the Security Council about the timing, objectives, and substance of a sanctions resolution in the near future.[51] The Clinton administration, which had undergone a series of diplomatic failures in Somalia, Bosnia, and Haiti, stood firm over the North Korean nuclear issue to recover the lost diplomatic points in those areas. In preparation for China's noncooperation in the United Nations, the United States considered independent sanctions with the help of its allies, the ROK and Japan. Furthermore, the United States was also deliberating on preemptive military strikes on the Yongbyon nuclear complex as Israel did on Iraq's Osiraq reactor in 1981.[52]

Neither Seoul nor Tokyo, however, were in a position to actively support Washington's sanctions option, not to speak of the air strike option, although in the end they reluctantly approved the sanctions option. South Korea, which had been attacked once by the North and whose people still remembered vividly the dreadful result of the war, was worried about the North retaliating against it, while Japan was concerned about the possible ineffectiveness of sanctions.[53] This may be recorded as a third dissonance between Seoul and Pyongyang.

The relations between Washington and Pyongyang became strained to the breaking point, while tensions on the Korean Peninsula reached the highest point since the beginning of the North Korean nuclear issue because the North, holding the South hostage, was warning that it would consider sanctions against it as an act of war. It seemed difficult to find a way out as both Washington and Pyongyang had become wary of each other. For its part, Washington was dismayed at Pyongyang's irrational actions and its continual breach of agreements to obtain more concessions. From the point of view of Pyongyang, the United States was unreasonable in its attempt to pressure North Korea with the threat of sanctions, since North Korea considered itself to have fulfilled its promise to Washington. Pyongyang seemed to think that the United States was placing hurdles one after another, hindering the third round of high-level talks whenever North Korea managed to jump a hurdle.[54] War on the Korean Peninsula seemed imminent, while peaceful resolution of the North Korean nuclear issue appeared virtually impossible.

The Fourth Phase (June 1994–October 1994):
From Stalemate to Breakthrough

Kim Il Sung, pushed into a corner, used a hidden card as he had done once before in late February when the negotiation between Pyongyang and the IAEA over the issue of regular inspections had reached a stalemate.[55] At that time, Billy Graham was picked. This time, he invited former U.S. President Jimmy Carter. During his visit from 15 to 18 June, Kim Il Sung told him that the reprocessing facility and a second reactor under construction would be opened for inspection only when North Korea was given a light-water reactor to replace its current reactor. In addition, the 82-year-old dictator told Carter that the North would freeze its nuclear program if given the light-water reactors. Second, the North Korean president demanded that the United States should guarantee the non-use of nuclear weapons against the North while hoping to hold the third round of negotiations with Washington to solve the nuclear issue.[56] Kim Il Sung also offered to meet his South Korean counterpart, Kim Young Sam. In this way, Carter made a breakthrough in the U.S.-North Korean standoff and played a major role in easing the tension on the Korean Peninsula to some extent. Carter's breakthrough was greeted with understandable skepticism in both Washington and Seoul, however, as the North's proposal was not specific and it had breached its promise several times in the past.

Amid the remaining tension on the Korean Peninsula, Kim Young Sam accepted Kim Il Sung's offer of a summit meeting on 20 June.[57] To overcome Washington's skepticism, Pyongyang on 22 June confirmed that it would freeze the major elements of its nuclear program as long as a new round of talks with Washington would proceed; in addition, it would not reload its 5MWe reactor with new fuel or reprocess spent fuel, and the IAEA would be allowed to keep its inspectors and monitoring equipment at the Yongbyon nuclear facility. In response, the State Department announced that the United States was ready to go forward with the third round of talks with Pyongyang in Geneva early in July and suspended the efforts to pursue a sanctions resolution in the U.N. Security Council.[58]

Finally, the third round of U.S.-North Korean negotiations resumed in Geneva, but in a surprising turn of events, the talks, which had been delayed for more than a year since the second round, had to be suspended just one day after the resumption. The sudden death of North Korea's "Great Leader" on 8 July put a stop to negotiations. Needless to say, the South-North summit meeting scheduled on 25-27 July had to be suspended as well. Washington and Pyongyang did resume talks five weeks later, and finally on 12 August, they reached agreement.[59] In a joint statement, the North agreed to freeze construction of the 50 MWe and 200 MWe reactors, forgo reprocessing, and seal the radiochemical laboratory to be monitored by the IAEA. In return, the United States agreed to arrange the replacement of the current graphite-moderated reactors with light-water reactors and provide interim energy alternatives until the reactors were in operation. In addition, the North agreed to remain a member of the NPT, while the United States agreed to establish diplomatic representation in Pyongyang. As agreed in the statement, in late September the two sides held additional expert-level discussions in Pyongyang and Berlin to specify the replacement of graphite-moderated reactors with light-water ones, the safe storage and disposal of the spent fuel, provision of alternative energy, and the establishment of liaison offices. U.S. and North Korean high-level negotiators met together again in Geneva, and after a month of difficult negotiations, they reached agreement. With final approval in the capitals of the two countries, on 21 October they signed a landmark Geneva Accord, which was composed of an agreed framework, a separate confidential document, and an appendix that is believed to be more specific.[60] The accord provided a road map to an overall solution to the nuclear issue of the Korean Peninsula through a comprehensive quid pro quo package deal as the North had persistently demanded.

From the perspective of the West, the agreement addresses all of the concerns about the problems of the past, present, and future involving North Korea's nuclear program. With respect to the past, North Korea agreed to the implementation of its full-scope safeguards agreement and whatever may be deemed necessary by the IAEA (including the special inspection of the two undeclared nuclear sites). The implementation must be completed before "key" nuclear components of one of the two light-water reactors are delivered. With respect to the present, the North agreed to freeze its 5 MWe graphite-moderated reactor and the reprocessing facility under the surveillance of the IAEA by 21 November, within one month of the agreement.[61] With respect to the future, Pyongyang agreed to dismantle the current nuclear facilities and the two large nuclear reactors: One is rated at 50 megawatts electric and the other at 200 megawatts electric, which would have produced hundreds of kilograms of plutonium annually if completed. It also agreed to ship the spent fuel taken out of the 5 MWe reactor— about 8,000 nuclear fuel rods, which would be a source of 25 to 30 kilograms of plutonium for four or five nuclear weapons—out of North Korea. In return, the United States agreed to arrange for construction of two new 1,000 MWe light-water nuclear reactors, valued at around $4-4.5 billion, to arrange the provision of an interim energy supply of 500,000 tons of heavy oil annually, pending completion of the first light-water reactor, provide negative security assurances, open liaison offices in Washington and Pyongyang, and lower trade barriers.

When the contents of the agreement became known, conservative critics said that the United States bought out the North Korean nuclear program, making a troubling precedent.[62] They argued that the deal might convince other nuclear aspirants such as Iran that they could use their secret nuclear weapons programs to bargain for major political and economic concessions.[63] Critics also argued that the deferment of the special inspection of the IAEA would spare time for the North to keep and export whatever nuclear weapons it had already built.[64]

The accord did not address only American concessions, however. North Korea not only agreed to remain a party to the NPT, it also agreed to allow the first-ever requested special inspection of the IAEA and to dismantle its own nuclear facilities, which it had developed for more than 20 years. In this sense, the nuclear deal between Washington and Pyongyang can hardly be seen as a "bad" precedent. Moreover, there are already similar "precedents" of American buyoff, which are not classified as negative; the United States has bought off other nuclear weapons as in Ukraine, financed Russian nuclear physicists lest they should sell their technology for money to rogue states, and purchased arms that have fallen into bad hands. Having done so, the United States used the logic that it is better to do a buyback than to have it fired at the United States.[65]

As far as the timing of the special inspection, there is no urgency in clarifying North Korea's past actions because there is no physical evidence that the North had produced enough plutonium or that it had developed one or two nuclear weapons with the reprocessed plutonium. There is great urgency, however, to prevent the North's repetition on a much larger scale. In this context, the United States did well by making North Korea's current and future threat a first priority and its uncertain past actions a second priority. Therefore, the U.S.-North Korean nuclear agreement will be the single most important foreign policy feat of the Clinton administration to date if it is ultimately carried out.[66]

189

IMPLEMENTATION OF THE AGREED FRAMEWORK

There is still a long way to go, however. The agreement is a joint venture of reciprocal steps that both sides would have to take in an almost decade-long implementation process, rotating through several stages with specific measures to be completed on specific dates. As the first joint step in implementing the agreed framework, the two sides have had to make a supply contract of the light-water reactor (hereinafter as LWR) to the North by 21 April 1995. At expert-level meetings in Berlin, however, representatives of the two countries could not reach an agreement on either the name of the LWR model or the prime contractor who would design, manufacture, construct, and manage the reactors, and so forth. With the target date of 21 April passing, North Korea threatened to renew its nuclear activities, such as reloading of the extracted 8,000 spent fuel rods unless its request were met. North Korea had fought against accepting the South Korean nuclear reactor model despite its promise of 21 October 1994, when it signed the Geneva Agreement, to accept the LWR from the South. Almost one month later from the time of the suspension of the expert-level negotiations, the United States and North Korea agreed to open semi-high level talks in Kuala Lumpur, Malaysia, from 19 May. The two sides, however, had much trouble in narrowing their different opinions. As for Pyongyang, it would be a matter of pride and regime survival to accept technologies and labors from its enemy, South Korea. On the other hand, the United States, in cooperation with South Korea, continued to urge North Korea to keep its previous promise.

Nonetheless, U.S. negotiators did not abandon hope, if small, to reach an agreement, seeing that North Korean negotiators seemed to make an effort to solve the LWR issue without mentioning such political matters as concluding a peace agreement with the United States as before. What made the United States and South Korea more optimistic was that North Korea gradually withdrew its insistence on the name of the LWR model and the prime contractor gradually as the negotiation continued. In exchange for the concessions, North Korea requested extra economic and technical assistance.

After more than three weeks of negotiations to narrow the gap, the two sides reached a compromise, which avoided a loss of face for North Korea but recognized South Korea's central role in providing LWRs to the North. The joint statement announced on 13 June 1995 never specifically stated South Korea as the provider, but a description in the statement made it clear that the source should only be South Korea.[67] In addition, the statement said that the United States would serve as the principal point of contact with North Korea and an American firm would serve as a program coordinator to supervise overall implementation of the LWR project. Concurrently, however, North Korea conceded that rather than the United States, the multinational consortium Korean Peninsula Energy Development Organization (KEDO), which was formed by South Korea, the United States, and Japan to carry out the terms of the Geneva Agreement, would select a prime contractor.[68] The new agreement reached in Kuala Lumpur was an important step toward implementing the Agreed Framework. As U.S. Ambassador-at-large Robert Gallucci stated, however, the Kuala Lumpur agreement will not be the last hurdle for the United States and South Korea to leap.[69]

CONCLUSION

It seems still too early to be optimistic about North Korea's promise to halt its nuclear program. Since North Korea has behaved against the international community's expectation by not keeping its promises in many cases, we may have to reserve optimism until the last moment concerning North Korea's real change in political, social, economic, and military spheres. Even in this widely open and rapidly changing world, North Korea still remains a hermit kingdom afraid of change.

It is fortunate, however, that a couple of small, but positive, signs with respect to Pyongyang's change are detected. North Korea is making efforts to induce foreign investments by opening wide the Rajin-Sonbong special economic zones to foreign countries. Moreover, the North agreed to receive 150,000 tons of rice from the South despite the fact that in accepting the rice, it loses face. South

Koreans are hoping that a friendly environment, which might be developed through the free rice shipments to the North, will help resume South-North talks, including the summit conference that was suspended due to the condolence issue involving the death of North Korea's Great Leader, Kim Il Sung, in July 1994. Improved relations between the South and the North will to a large extent help solve the North Korean nuclear issue and further develop peace and stability in Northeast Asia.

As we have known through the entire process of the nuclear deal between North Korea and the United States, however, North Korea has been doing its best to exclude South Korea in negotiations. The North does not want political contacts with the South, which may not react favorably on the North Korean regime. What the North wants from the South is economic assistance, which will alleviate North Korean people's discontent derived from food shortages. Pyongyang is busy contacting Americans and the Japanese. Pyongyang is well aware that improving relations with the United States and Japan will produce a great deal of political and economic gains. Kim Jong Il can make the most of such political and economic gains from former enemies and thus strengthen his power over both people and party officials by establishing liaison offices, introducing free rice and oil, and then publicizing that all of the achievements are the results of his brilliant leadership.

North Korea, however, should understand that efforts to gain recognition from the United States and Japan, excluding South Korea, will face joint opposition from the three countries. No matter what they really want from Pyongyang, both Washington and Tokyo would not try to make friends with Pyongyang so long as the latter persists in its policy not to contact the South. Therefore, North Korea, if it really wants survival, has to begin negotiations with no other than South Korea. The North may allay concerns about its nuclear program by developing on a mutually acceptable basis a nuclear inspection regime through the Joint Nuclear Control Committee meetings with the South. The transparency of the North Korean nuclear program will also be assured through faithful implementation of the Geneva Agreed Framework at each scheduled stage. Only in this way can Pyongyang solve the nuclear issue and achieve economic recovery and political stability through international recognition.

ENDNOTES

1. The Americans presented their concerns to the former Soviet Union, which had supported North Korea's civilian nuclear program and had worked closely with the United States to limit the spread of nuclear weapons capability.

2. This bit of history is significant because it helps explain why Pyongyang asked Washington to provide light-water reactors in high-level talks. See Selig S. Harrison, "The North Korean Nuclear Crisis: From Stalemate to Breakthrough," *Arms Control Today*, November 1994, 19.

3. In June 1978, the United States issued a general negative security assurance, pledging not to use nuclear weapons against any nonnuclear weapons state that was a party to the NPT unless such a state attacked the United States, its armed forces, or one of its allies and was itself allied to a nuclear weapons state. Pyongyang would not accept the general NSA, however. It turned out to be only a tactic of Pyongyang to draw political gains out of engagement with Washington.

4. *FBIS*, EAS-91-189, 30 September 1991, 11-12.

5. This may show that pragmatists and technocrats of the North Korean Worker's Party, who have argued that a changing international environment requires major changes in North Korean policy, won a victory at that time over hard-liners, who had warned that Seoul, Washington, and Tokyo would seek to exploit the vulnerability of the North. *See* Selig S. Harrison, "The North Korean Nuclear Crisis: From Stalemate to Breakthrough," 18-19.

6. The North also argued that on the assumption that the United States, which had the right to decide on nuclear weapons in South Korea, would announce a clear position, Pyongyang would sign the nuclear safeguards accord. See *FBIS*, EAS-91-246, 23 December 1991, 11.

7. The joint U.S.-South Korean "Team Spirit" military exercises, begun in 1976 and among the largest in the world, included simulated nuclear attacks on North Korea throughout the 1980s and as recently as 1993. *See* Martin Hart-Landsberg, "Who's Threatening Who?," *Technological Review,* July 1994, 72-73.

8. The unprecedented request of a special inspection was made possible through revitalization of the IAEA in the wake of the Gulf War. Being shocked by the secret Iraqi nuclear development program, which had gone undetected by routine IAEA inspections of declared nuclear sites until the series of United Nations–sponsored special inspections on suspected facilities revealed the fact, the international community agreed to strengthen the nonproliferation regime in order to block nuclear proliferation with all means available. *See* Gary Samore, "Iraq," in Mitchell Reiss and Robert S. Littwak (eds.), *Nuclear Proliferation after the Cold War* (Washington, D.C.: Woodrow Wilson Center, 1994), 19-24.

9. Andrew Mack, "Security and the Korean Peninsula in the 1990s," in Andrew Mack (ed.), *Asian Flashpoint: Security and the Korean Peninsula* (Canberra: Allen & Unwin, 1993), 4.

10. Although meetings of the Joint Commission held 13 rounds, both sides could not narrow the gap with respect to the concept of mutual inspection. South Korea argued that inspections based on reciprocity and inspections without sanctuary should be conducted to establish a reliable and effective bilateral inspection regime, whereas North Korea contested that inspections based on mutual concerns and inspections of the U.S. military bases in the South should be carried out.

11. James C. Wendt, *The North Korean Nuclear Program: What is to be Done?* (Santa Monica: Rand, 1994), 3-4.

12. Withdrawal from the NPT is not an illegal action. According to article X of the treaty, each party has the right to withdraw from the treaty if it decides that extraordinary events have jeopardized the supreme interests of its country.

13. Spurgeon M. Keeny, "The North Korean Crisis," *Arms Control Today*, May 1993, 2.

14. Even when Pyongyang announced the decision to withdraw from the NPT, it left room to return to the treaty if the United States changed its hostile stance against the North. The statement said, "Our principled stance will *not* change *before* the United States suspends the nuclear threat against us and the IAEA Secretariat returns to principles of independence and fairness. The United States should immediately suspend the Team Spirit military exercise and renounce its maneuvers to plot to harm and obliterate nonnuclear countries by manipulating the IAEA." *See* "Statement Notes Withdrawal," *FBIS*, EAS-93-047, 12 March 1993, 18-19. Right after the announcement of the statement, the North Korean government made its ambassadors abroad and high-ranking officials reiterate the necessity of the U.S.-North Korean talks to solve the nuclear issue in an interview with foreign reporters. Moreover, the North Korean Foreign Ministry also demanded the negotiation between the United States and North Korea in a statement. *Pyongyang Times*, 27 April 1993, 7.

15. *See* "U.N. Security Council Resolution 825 on the North Korean Nuclear Issue," *U.S. Department of State Dispatch*, 24 May 1993, 383.

16. Hakjoon Kim, *Unification Policies of South and North Korea, 1945-1991: A Comparative Study* (Seoul: Seoul National University Press, 1992), 359-60.

17. Daniel Russel, "U.S.-North Korean Relations," in Man-Woo Lee (ed.), *Current Issues in Korean-U.S. Relations: Korean American Dialogue* (Seoul: The Institute for Far Eastern Studies, Kyungnam University, 1993), 45.

18. Arnold Kanter, "North Korea, Nuclear Proliferation, and U.S. Policy: Collective Engagement in a New Era," a Statement Before a Hearing of the Subcommittee on East Asia and Pacific Foreign Affairs Committee, U.S. Senate on 6 February 1992, 16.

19. By inserting the NSA phrase in the joint statement, North Korea could show internally and externally that its insistent demand had been fulfilled, and the United States should be responsible for the initiation of the nuclear issue on the Korean Peninsula.

20. *New York Times*, 12 June 1993. For the full text of the joint statement, see *FBIS*, EAS-93-112, 14 June 1993, 13.

21. See "Kang Sok-Ju Holds News Conference," *FBIS*, EAS-93-112, 14 June 1993, 13-14.

22. *New York Times*, 12 June 1993, 1.

23. A light-water reactor that uses light (ordinary) water to moderate the speed of neutrons is the more proliferation-resistant reactor compared to a heavy-water or a graphite moderated reactor in that in the light-water reactor none of the fissile material entering or leaving the plant is directly usable in a nuclear weapon. For more information about the nuclear fuel cycle or the characteristics of reactors, *see* Gary T. Gardner, *Nuclear Nonproliferation—A Primer* (London: Lynne Rinner Publishers, 1994), chap. 1-3.

24. According to a South Korean government official, Kang Sok-Ju had proposed to Gallucci the replacement of North Korea's reactor type at the luncheon meeting held shortly after the first round of talks ended on 12 June. Kang, the official said, reportedly told Gallucci that it was the will of Kim Il Sung. Gallucci seemed to pay little attention to Kang's remarks, however, so when delegates of the North proposed to the U.S. side the reactor conversion option at the second session of the Geneva talks, U.S. delegates were not so well prepared to answer the offer at the session. Three days later at another session, they accepted the offer of North Korea. See *FBIS*, EAS-93-137, 20 July 1993, 34.

25. For the full text of the joint statement, see *FBIS*, EAS-93-137, 20 July 1993, 33.

26. *New York Times*, 20 July 1993, A2. His description of "small"

progress can be interpreted as the United States having failed to persuade North Korea to allow a special inspection of the two suspected sites of nuclear material. The "significant" progress may be understood to indicate that the United States was successful in bringing North Korea back on track of negotiation with the IAEA and South Korea.

27. Robert L. Gallucci, "U.S.-North Korea Talks on the Nuclear Issue," *U.S. Department of State Dispatch*, 26 July 1993, 535-36.

28. Jon B. Wolfsthal, "North Korea Suspends IAEA Talks; Seeks Dialogue with Washington," *Arms Control Today*, November 1993, 21.

29. For the full text, see *FBIS*, EAS-93-217, 12 November 1993, 19-21.

30. So far, Washington had maintained the principle that the third round of high-level talks would not be held unless the North would implement the full-scope safeguards agreement with the IAEA, including special inspection of the two suspected nuclear sites, and would resume talks with South Korea for making an effective bilateral inspection regime. Welcoming North Korea's package deal offer under which the North renounces its nuclear program in exchange for security guarantees and diplomatic and economic benefits, however, the United States discarded a step-by-step approach to which close interlocutors of the United States, South Korea, and Japan had clung.

31. Nayan Chanda, "Fission Chips Down," *Far Eastern Economic Review*, 2 December 193, 16-17.

32. Nayan Chanda, "Divided Counsel," *Far Eastern Economic Review*, 16 December 1993, 16.

33. The reason for North Korea's refusal on this scope was its claim that as a member who had not rejoined the NPT, it did not need to abide by all the provisions of the treaty.

34. IAEA Director-General Hans Blix called Pyongyang's argument "a la carte-ism," in which nations subject to the

agency's monitoring try to negotiate which inspections they would allow and which they would not. He compared that to a tourist telling a customs inspector which piece of luggage he could open.

35. After its inspectors were restricted to such minor maintenance work as changing batteries and film in monitoring cameras when they visited North Korea in August, the IAEA said it would send no more missions there unless they would be free to make all the checks they wanted.

36. *FBIS*, EAS-94-021, 1 February 1994, 18-19.

37. Paul Lewis, "U.S. Urges China to Pressure North Koreans to Open Nuclear Sites," *New York Times*, 6 February 1994, 6.

38. *FBIS*, EAS-94-021, 1 February 1994, 35.

39. Among the press reports that upset Seoul was a detailed scenario of a second Korean War in the *New York Times* on 6 February, two weeks before the deadline. The war scenario said that if another war broke out on the Korean Peninsula, there would be hundreds of thousands of casualties on each side, not including civilians, and there would be a fierce counteroffensive intended to seize Pyongyang and to topple the government of Kim Il Sung.

40. Susumu Awanohara, "Hawks Alight," *Far Eastern Economic Review*, 24 February 1994, 23-24.

41. David E. Sanger, "North Koreans Agree to Survey of Atomic Sites," *New York Times*, 16 February 1994, A1.

42. *U.S. Department of State Dispatch*, 14 March 1994, 151.

43. Lynn E. Davis, "Nuclear Situation in North Korea," *U.S. Department of State Dispatch*, 21 March 1994, 165-67.

44. J. F. O. McAllister, "Pyongyang's Dangerous Game," *Time*, 4 April 1994, 60-61.

45. In a sense, this allegation is true because China's influence has certainly waned since it normalized relations with South Korea

and turned down some of North Korea's previous requests for more arms and aid. However, no one doubts that China has the power not to protect the economically decrepit Kim Il Sung regime from sanctions. Their own difficult relations with America over MFN status and human rights to some extent irked the Chinese and tempted them to tilt toward the North Koreans. *See* "Beijing Ducks," *Far Easter Economic Review*, 7 April 1994, 5. "China's Choice," *Economist*, 9 April 1994, 15-16. Laxmi Nakarmi, "Why Clinton Can't Use a Big Stick on North Korea," *Business Week*, 4 April 1994, 51.

46. R. Jeffrey Smith, "South Korea Offers Gesture to North," *Washington Post*, 16 April 1994.

47. The earlier U.S. position was doubtless based on the assumption that if the South-North talks progress over the nuclear issue and make an efficient inspection regime, it would be very helpful to assure the transparency of North Korea's nuclear program with the implementation of full-scope safeguards of the IAEA. With this hope in mind, the United States demanded significant progress of the South-North talks for further talks with the North. The South-North talks did not develop at all, however, and few hoped the two sides would make a breakthrough. Now that things had come to this, the United States seemed to have decided to discard the South-North talks option before resuming the third round of high-level talks with the North because it was no longer a card, but a burden. Washington was being caught in a bid of Seoul, however, and wanting not to be left behind in the contacts between Washington and Pyongyang, Seoul had insisted that the South-North talks had to produce significant outcomes before the U.S.-North Korean talks resumed.

48. The examination could help resolve the mystery of a 100-day shutdown of the reactor in 1989, when U.S. intelligence believes fuel rods were taken out and reprocessed into enough weapons-grade plutonium to make one or two Nagasaki-sized bombs. Nayan Chanda, "Forgive and Forget?," *Far Eastern Economic Review*, 12 May 1994, 14-15.

49. "Selective Chronology Regarding Safeguards in the DPRK," *IAEA Newsbriefs*, July/August 1994, 3.

50. "Resolution on DPRK Safeguards Adopted by the Board on 10 June 1994," *IAEA Newsbriefs*, July/August 1994, 2.

51. Bruce W. Nelan, "Down the Risky Path," *Time*, 13 June 1994, 24-28.

52. At a hearing of the Senate Foreign Affairs Committee held in January 1995, Secretary of Defense William Perry testified that the United States was seriously considering an air raid on Yongbyon nuclear facilities during late May and early June 1994. *Hankuk Ilbo* (Washington edition), 28 January 1995. It was early April that Perry made a public remark about the preemptive military strike option against the North. He said the Clinton administration was not considering a preemptive military strike "at that time and under these circumstances. I am not ruling that option out in the future." *See* Jeffrey Smith, "Perry Warns of Strong Pressure to Halt North Korean A-Arms Plan," *Washington Post*, 4 April 1995, A15.

53. The massive flow of funds from the pro-Pyongyang Korean community in Japan to North Korea is estimated at $600-$1,600 million per year. That is the North's major source of financial support. A couple of administrative orders from the Finance Ministry would block direct money transfers from Japan to North Korea. If direct remittances from Japan were blocked, however, the money could easily be routed through a third country such as Hong Kong. *See* Charles Smith, "Ifs and Buts of Sanctions," *Far Eastern Economic Review*, 16 June 1994, 16.

54. One of the North Korean diplomats described Washington's demand as follows: A man (the U.S.) and a woman (the North) has plans to get married. The man was so anxious to know the chastity of his partner that he tried to have her take off her clothes. She, who is a virgin, was ashamed, but took her outer clothes off. He was not satisfied, however, and demanded that she take one more garment off. She reluctantly agreed. He still was not satisfied and tried to strip her.

Under these circumstances, how can she, who has already been humiliated, accept such a reckless demand?

55. Besides Kim Il Sung, North Korean high-ranking officials, including Kim Yong-Sun and Kang Sok-Ju, used visiting Americans who were influential in American political and academic fields as a communication channel through which the North Koreans revealed their intentions tacitly and suggested a condition for compromise with the United States whenever Pyongyang and the United States reached an impasse. This unofficial communication channel used by the North is evaluated as being very useful in reading Pyongyang's bottom line.

56. Jimmy Carter, "Report of Our Trip to Korea," *Hankuk Ilbo* (Washington edition), 11 October 1994.

57. Jae Hoon Shim, "Not All Smiles," *Far Eastern Economic Review*, 30 June 1994, 16.

58. Robert L. Gallucci, "North Korea Nuclear Situation," *U.S. Department of State Dispatch*, 27 June 1994, 421.

59. Alan Riding, "U.S. and N. Korea Say They'll Seek Diplomatic Links," *New York Times*, 13 August 1994, 1.

60. Alan Riding, "U.S. and North Korea Sign Pact to End Nuclear Dispute," *New York Times*, 22 October 1994. The United States seems to have been very anxious to keep the agreement. As a goodwill gesture, after approving the agreement, President Clinton addressed on 20 October a so-called "letter of assurance" to Kim Jong Il, who had not yet been officially named the late Kim's successor, confirming Washington's commitment to the accord.

61. In compliance with the agreement, North Korea did not restart the reactor and sealed the reprocessing facility in November 1994.

62. R. Jeffrey Smith, "N. Korea Accord: A Troubling Precedent?," *Washington Post*, 20 October 1994.

63. Ibid. In reality, top Iranian officials were reported to have complained to the IAEA Board of Governors in September that the country had received little reward for its complete cooperation with the agency's inspection requests and to have hinted that its leaders might decide to withdraw from the NPT regime if more benefits were not forthcoming.

64. Caspar W. Weinberger, "The Appeasement of North Korea," *Forbes*, 21 November 1994, 35.

65. Michael Kramer, "A Tough, Smart Deal," *Time*, 31 October 1994, 34.

66. Jessica Mathews, "A Sound Beginning with North Korea," *Washington Post*, 21 October 1994, A25.

67. The joint statement states that the LWR project will "consist of two pressurized light-water reactors with two coolant loops . . . currently under construction," which refers to Ulchin 3 and 4, the Korean standard nuclear power plant model. For the full text of the joint statement, see *Korea Herald*, 14 June 1995, 2.

68. T. R. Reid and Lee Keumhyun, "S. Korea Accepts Deal With North on A-Power," *Washington Post*, 14 June 9195, A32.

69. Andrew Pollack, "South Korea Likely to Build New Reactors," *New York Times*, 14 June 1995, A5.